"The book that changed my life w Testament. Romans is about the position in Christ, and manifesting His glory within us once we become new creatures. There was a time that the Lord had me read Romans 6, 7, and 8 every day until I learned the power of self, sin, and triumphant glory. Becky Castle has taught the book of Romans for many years. She now has developed those teachings into an incredible book that can accelerate you in embracing who you are in Christ. *The Exchange: Surrender to the Process* is a path to freedom and fullness that I would highly recommend to anyone."

—**Dr. Chuck D. Pierce**,
President, Glory of Zion International Ministries;
President, Global Spheres, Inc.

"From fullness to fulfillment—this always was God's ultimate divine design for our lives! Then our life in a fallen world disrupted His plan. As believers in Christ, we need a template of how to exchange the bombardment of daily demonic lies for eternal godly truths. The book of Romans was the pinnacle of Paul's New Testament writings. This in-depth template from the Word of God is the core of Becky Castle's life teaching. As you read *The Exchange* with intentionality, you, too, will experience old mindsets shift, new freedoms spring up in your heart, and the birth of greater hopes and dreams. May the joy of oneness with our Creator become an attainable reality in your life as you apply these timeless truths and enjoy the journey of surrender."

—**Jill Mitchell O'Brien**,
President/Founder,
Kingdom Connections International,
www.kingdomconnectionsintl.com

"In *The Exchange*, Becky Castle writes, 'Adam and Eve were already like God, being made in His image, but they were tempted to be like Him *without* Him. We have the same issue.' In today's world, discerning lies from the truth has become a national and global obsession. Yet for many people, challenges and even despair have only increased when the scope of a truth is revealed. That's because only in Jesus will the truth actually make you free. As our pioneering friend Becky Castle shares, you can learn to exchange lies for truth in a way that transforms your life. Be prepared—this book is a deep dive into God's heart and yours. With gentle hilarity and the skill of a surgeon, our friend Becky Castle will teach you to gain the freedom and fullness in life you've always known you could attain. There's no more crucial time than now."

—**Jon and Jolene Hamill**,
Lamplighter Ministries

"This powerful book provides important information from the Bible for practical Christian living. My personal life has been impacted by Becky Castle and the message of *The Exchange*. She has written a book that is simple to understand. It is a book for anyone who finds themselves in 'a stuck place.'"

—**Apostle Maggie Carrasquillo**,
Passion, Fire and Love Ministries

"The very title of this book, *The Exchange: Surrender to the Process, a Romans-Based Path to Freedom and Fullness*, immediately drew my attention as I'm continually in awe of the Great Exchange provided through the amazing, great, and abounding grace of God for us.

Becky Castle has clearly articulated the importance of recognizing the strongholds that can keep us from walking in the fullness and freedom provided for us, and from discovering God's intent and design in life. She reminds us that the truths of the gospel can be applied practically to every situation so we may understand the intimacy God desires for us and with us. We can break the cycles of blame and shame that keep us from experientially knowing the love of God!

In this book, I was also personally encouraged and reminded of the liberation, freedom, and power we have through authentic worship and devotion.

This quote from Becky Castle's book says it well: 'To worship God means that we abandon our own understanding, our own rules, and our own way of living and give Him our attention and affection, yielding to Him as the truth. This Exchange message is ultimately about making the choice to yield to God. God is the only One worthy of our worship. He is the only Righteous One who created us and redeemed us because He loves us so.'"

—**Doug Stringer**,
Somebody Cares America,
Somebody Cares International

"I have known Becky Castle for over 20 years. I have heard her teach what she has written in this book. It is a powerful tool that has great potential to set captives free, open blind eyes, and bring into focus many of the biblical truths we have been taught. Becky has a way of taking the familiar, digging into it, and finding gold. I highly recommend this book. You will discover life-changing truths that will impact your journey into Christlikeness."

—**Regina Shank**,
Global Transformation International,
Regina Shank Ministries

"Becky Castle systematically assimilates the Word of God in the *The Exchange*, presenting a full-course menu that is inherently rich with godly insights and inclusive of wholesome spiritual ingredients to nourish your body, soul, and spirit."

—Rajesh Y. Nath,
Kingdom Consultant and Founder,
Father's Love International Ministries

BECKY CASTLE

The Exchange
SURRENDER TO THE PROCESS

A Romans-Based Path to Freedom and Fullness

LUCIDBOOKS

To Bob and Lynda Hansard, Rollin DeLap,
and Jack Taylor, who modeled for me
that faith in Jesus Christ and His Word is
preeminent above every other thing.

TABLE OF CONTENTS

FOREWORD

Becky Castle has been a mentor and godly example to my husband, Eric, and me for over twenty-five years. Walking with her daily throughout these past years, in the valleys and on the heights, has revealed her proven character, knowledge of the truth, and closeness with God.

I met Becky in 1991 while she was the missions director at Southwest Baptist University. Through her Bible studies and our time together, I began to see the power of Christ at work in my life, which produced a hunger to know Him more and set a course of intimacy with Him in my everyday life.

In 1995, Becky initiated a gathering of like-hearted people who desired to meet regularly to worship and pray together. It was at this time that Becky and Eric's connection began. Our times together involved asking the Holy Spirit questions and sharing among the group what we were hearing and seeing. Romans 12:1–2 became evident in our weekly Acts 2-type worship and prayer times. We became a body of radical worshippers experiencing His presence, and hearing and obeying Him, we were transformed. Consequently, this laid a strong foundation for a church plant and later a ministry where we partnered and served with her on staff.

Among the church body, Becky became known as a threshing sledge—or by some, a "but kicker" (spelling intended). Her ability to speak the truth in love divided out the "buts" we often offer the Lord and replaced it with a yielding to His Spirit, allowing the seed to be separated from the chaff. This made room for repentance and His fullness to be revealed. We all kept coming back for more. To see a plumb line dropped with Christ as the cornerstone was refreshing, and Becky's authenticity produced in all of us a desire for more.

Becky's Exchange teaching from Romans exhorts us all to walk in the fullness of God. This lifestyle teaching is what she has lived and demonstrated from the first day we met her. It starts with divine communion with the Father, giving Him our "stuck places," lack, and the lies we believed to exchange with the truth of our identity in Him.

This book's message will open the eyes of your heart to understand how *"the hope of His calling"* (Eph 1:17–19) that Paul writes about means that *everything* in your life has a time for redemption and complete restoration. No matter what you have done or what has been done to you, you can be fully restored through the Exchange message. Furthermore, this book's message will help you understand that God has His own possession of inheritance in you that He desires to reap for Himself. His miraculous power, appropriated through the cross of Christ, is toward you as you believe.

The book emphasizes the religious trap that many Christians fall into when they explore only the beginning edges of their salvation, as if choosing to live in the foyer of a large mansion. We are invited to walk in the fullness that He has offered us. As His children, we can greatly expect the revealing of His glory.

An example of Becky's labor of discipleship and the invitation for more in our lives came in 2008 when Eric and I experienced His fullness at work in our marriage. After sharing with Becky a place of great conflict between us, we engaged the Holy Spirit with her by asking Him to reveal the root issues of the marital problems. He was faithful to reveal the lies we believed that were producing independence and even rebellion in each of our identities as married partners. Yielding to Him, we exercised the gift of repentance, and He revealed to us a glorious truth that we are under His divine covering of joy with the fruits of the Spirit accessible to us even in our conflicts. That became a pinnacle breakthrough for our marriage.

As a result of the countless encounters with the Lord in the Exchange message, a legacy of the gospel at work has multiplied to our children. Both of our daughters became attuned to the Enemy's lies and the cares of this world that they were entertaining at an early age. In response, they have been able to exchange the lies for the truth of what the Holy Spirit says about their identities in Christ. This is a direct result of Becky's teaching.

We recommend Becky with great confidence to be the teacher that leads you into the reality of God's love and redemptive purpose for your life. Traveling with Becky— whether in America, Bosnia, Mexico, or the United Kingdom— we have seen firsthand how the Exchange message transcends cultures and transforms lives.

The Exchange message and the principles of the how-tos found in this book will give you the biblical permission to believe in and experience the power of the cross daily. This message will bring you into a deeper knowledge of the One who loves you in the past, present, and future.

We urge you to take the time to enrich yourself with the revelation of this message, which will empower your daily walk with Him.

Eric and Rebecca Vaughn

PREFACE

I have been in Christian ministry for forty-two years. That includes youth ministry, student work on Baptist university campuses, missionary work in China, leading women's Bible studies, and starting two churches. I currently lead an apostolic ministry called Launch Houston, which is part of an apostolic network I started in 2005 called Cornelius Connection International, supporting works in Bosnia, Scotland, and Fort Worth, Texas. Twenty years ago, I heard the Lord say to me on a return trip from Bosnia that if someone could network the networks, they could take a nation. Cornelius Connection is my effort to do that.

Many years ago, I began to understand what a life lived by the Spirit was all about, but before that, I was raised a Methodist, served in the Baptist denomination for many years, and worked alongside Lutherans and nondenominational ministries, among other groups. I have a great appreciation for the strengths in each of these.

But let me back up a bit. I come from a middle-class American family. I have two sisters. My parents provided a basically stable home, although they fought a lot and didn't know how to reconcile much of anything. Living in a home with a good bit of anger in it and not much reconciliation was disturbing to me because I had a high need for peace. I spent a lot of time alone in my room, struggling with anger and in distress over my family's dysfunction.

I was raised on a street full of neighborhood boys, and I loved sports, so we were always playing one game or another. Eventually, I played for school and city leagues. But playing with the boys on my street wasn't all fun and games. I was given many opportunities to learn how to defend myself. For example, I was afraid of storms because when there were any clouds in the sky, a neighbor lady would tell me tornados were coming. Once when I was at a neighbor's house, it began to rain hard, and I wanted to go home. The boys locked the gate and wouldn't let me leave. Another time, one of the boys chased me around my yard with a machete! Fear motivated me to learn how to defend myself and my younger sister.

My family went to a church that gave us a foundation about God, Jesus Christ, and His love for us but never really explained how to have a personal relationship with Him. Never did I hear about our need to be born again. I wasn't taught in my childhood church that each of us could live a life of fullness in Him. Mostly the preacher spoke about being a good person. I struggled with anger, so that didn't sit well with me.

It's amazing what the Lord uses to be the foundation for our destiny. Now it is so clear to me that He designed me to reconcile people to each other and, more importantly, to Him. The angst I had in my home life positioned me to search for a way to overcome the stress and disappointment I lived with for most of my growing-up years.

I can remember sitting in a church service when I was about thirteen years old, wondering about the message I was hearing. Listening to those preachers, I was frustrated. I looked around me at the great people in that church, good-hearted people, but I did not see the level of power and authority I saw in the Bible. In my own understanding, I thought, *If God sent His Son to die on the cross to take our sins on Him and then was raised from the dead, if He did powerful miracles while on earth, then where is this power in people's lives today?*

I had felt for years a "knowing" of God but was left wondering how He was actually involved in my life. Then one day in a youth meeting, I had an encounter with His presence that was beyond natural. I felt His holiness and His love all at once. That was the moment I knew He was the truest reality of all of life and that I was in desperate need of knowing Him.

That day changed everything. What I had known through religion paled in light of experiencing Him. I propelled myself onto a journey to discover what it would mean to be His and to give myself to Him. I was literally transformed from being a person who knows *about* God to being a child *of* God who longed to know Him. Since that day, my life has been yielded to His life.

Over the next few years of high school, the Lord surrounded me with mentors who taught me how to be with God daily through scripture and prayer. I found myself hungry to be in His Word and to get understanding of what it meant to be a believer. I began to ask questions about how the life, death, and resurrection of Christ affected my daily life.

I read books by Watchman Nee and Jeanne Guyon, and the devotional book *My Utmost for His Highest* by Oswald Chambers. They all wrote about the transformational power of Christ.

Romans 6:4 says, *"Therefore we have been buried with Him through baptism into death, so that, just as Christ was raised from the dead through the glory of the Father, so we too might walk in newness of life.*" This verse helped me realize that my new life was to be hidden in Christ's and that I could somehow yield to His life in me, causing Him to manifest His life through me. I spent a lot of time in the book of Romans as well as the letters to the churches (Galatians, Ephesians, Philippians, Colossians, and so on).

Romans 3:9–26 had a profound impact on me because it explains the whole process of becoming a believer. That's what happened to me in that youth service when I understood that only God could fully satisfy the need of my life to be made whole. I could choose to stop trying to be good or right or okay and instead receive His gift of rightness through His Son, Jesus Christ, who was already right and just.

Throughout college and into my early twenties, it became clear to me that the Lord had a call on my life for the ministry. I became a youth minister. The ways of God are mysterious! When I was a youth, the Lord met me so strongly, and the very questions I had been asking I now wanted to help youth discover for themselves. The revelations I've shared with you up to this point in my life began to be real to me in so many ways. Others now needed me to train them. This brought a new level of freedom and authority to me that I didn't have before. God used the difficulties I had been through to train me, and I became more of who God made me to be.

I was regularly encountering people who already believed in Christ or who knew they needed Him but had no idea how to live for Him. I would share these beginning truths, and we would study the Bible a lot. It was easy to see His nature of love, kindness, and peace, but it was harder to know how to live like Him. I loved sharing with others the life-giving revelations I was learning.

I continued to study Watchman Nee. There is a diagram in his book *The Spiritual Man* that describes our being as having three parts: body, soul, and spirit (1 Thess. 5:23). You'll read more about this later in the book. This diagram helped me understand that when I was born again in Christ, my spirit that had been dead to God came alive to Him.

[T]hat He would grant you, according to the riches of His glory, to be strengthened with power through His Spirit in the inner man, so that Christ may dwell in your hearts through faith; and that you, being rooted and grounded in love, may be able to comprehend with all the saints what is the breadth and length and height and depth, and to know the love of Christ which surpasses knowledge, that you may be filled up to all the fullness of God.

—Eph. 3:16–19

These verses . . . unbelievable! The God of the universe loves me so much that according to His riches (I'm still learning the fullness of this), He is strengthening me by His Spirit living in me so I can live in all His fullness, filled up with knowing Him in every situation in life! Who wants to live another way?

Fullness—what does that mean, what does it look like, and how do I engage it? This became my pursuit as I was trying to help others. The more I grew in knowing Him and His lavish heart toward me, the more my hunger increased to give up everything else that would hinder this life of fullness. I began to search out the nature and ways of God—His character and how He moves about. This whole journey was a learning curve in redemption, restoration, and forgiveness. To have fullness, you cannot live in the bondage of wounds, lack, and unforgiveness.

As I counseled people during this season of my life, the Lord revealed simple diagrams for me to use to illustrate in practical ways the truths of daily life in God. You will see these in the chapters of this book. I have watched these practical illustrations help people grasp the process of living an Exchanged life.

This process of relating to God is what has become known as "The Exchange." Proverbs 3:5-6 says, *"Trust in the LORD with all your heart and do not lean on your own understanding. In all your ways acknowledge Him, and He will make your paths straight."* John 15:4 says, *"Abide in Me, and I in you. As the branch cannot bear fruit of itself unless it abides in the vine, so neither can you unless you abide in Me."* These verses along with many others confirmed that I needed to live a life of exchange—exchanging lies for God's truth.

Wherever I was not experiencing the fullness of God in my life, I must have been believing lies. Fullness means lacking nothing. I wanted to live a life of fullness, so I became resolute to know God in every situation so I could line up with His truth and ways.

God is redemptive and restorative, and He truly wants fullness for us. I believe that no matter what life has dealt or will deal us, we can choose for God to come into those situations and show us the truth instead of the lies we have believed. As we agree with the truth of God, who is Lord over everything, we can turn away from the lies that this world and the Enemy want us to be entrapped by, and we can step into the fullness of Christ in our innermost being. That is freedom!

When we see the difference between how the fallenness of this world has shaped us and the kind intentions of our

Father God, we can exchange the pain, lies, and shallow way of living for the lengths and heights and depths of the love of Christ that surpasses knowledge so we can be filled up with His fullness. That is a redeemed life.

As I read God's Word, there are so many promises of who He is, how He loves, and what He has in store for us. Before I knew these truths, I longed to apprehend them—to know God is eternal life, a life that is beyond this world and full of everything that is in heaven. I longed to know joy, peace, truth, overcoming, satisfaction, provision, dreams, power, forgiveness, hope, faith, confidence, and fullness.

To help you surrender to the process of living an Exchanged life, I've included at the end of each chapter a few key verses and instructions for growth, along with a prayer to decree. These are an important step to getting you into a deeper relationship with God and will help you engage the truth on a deep, personal level. My hope for you is that as you read this book, your hunger for God will abound, your confidence in His love for you will inspire you to great trust, and your faith will increase so you can risk vulnerability with Him and be known to the fullest.

One final note: I love sports, I drink iced black tea every day, I would have been a comedian if I had not been called to ministry, I don't take life or myself too seriously (not that it's not serious but because it is), and I choose to laugh a lot and give others a lot of freedom.

Enjoy the truths in this book. It is a lot, but God's got you!

Becky Castle

Chapter 1

THE FULLNESS OF GOD

[A]nd that you, being rooted and grounded in love, may be able to comprehend with all the saints what is the breadth and length and height and depth, and to know the love of Christ which surpasses knowledge, that you may be filled up to all the fullness of God.

—Eph. 3:17–19

Y ou were created to live a life you have yet to live. God's perfect plan from the beginning of creation was for you to enjoy unhindered communion with Him and bring purpose, joy, love, peace, companionship, and fulfillment through knowing Him and having an ongoing relationship with Him. This is worship. The reason you long to be loved unconditionally and completely by someone is because you were made for that to be the reality of your life. You were made to wholeheartedly love God in response to His wholehearted love for you.

When God created the earth and filled it with all the living things, it was His intention for mankind to rule over the earth from the place of complete fulfillment because their identity was firmly rooted in His love. God called this good. Adam and Eve were made in God's image; His nature was their nature. They had open communion with the Creator and with each other.

The realm of God—life in the Spirit—is love, joy, peace, patience, kindness, goodness, faithfulness, gentleness, and self-control. There is no death, no pain, no mourning, and no crying. There is light all around—no darkness is there. There is no sin, no unbelief, no lack, no impurity, no murder, no immorality, no witchcraft, and no idolatry. Nothing impure will ever enter it. There is fruitfulness, healing, and eternal life. That is how God intended life with Him to be lived.

God's Original Intent

God's heart is to have communion with a people who long to co-labor with Him in His nature and ways. In Genesis 1:26–28, we read:

> Then God said, "Let Us make man in Our image, according to Our likeness; and let them rule over the fish of the sea and over the birds of the sky and over the cattle and over all the earth, and over every creeping thing that creeps on the earth." So God created man in His own image, in the image of God He created him; male and female He created them. God blessed them; and God said to them, "Be fruitful and multiply, and fill the earth, and subdue it."

God made mankind in His image and imparted to us the likeness to live in His character, His nature, and His life, and then to fill the earth, releasing His rule and His reign. Nothing of the ways of this world is supposed to rule over us or in us. When we are one with Jesus, we should be radiating the glory and beauty of God everywhere we go. We're not created to be orphans, doing life on our own. We're not just wounded people. We are to be the children of God, lovers of God, one with Him. That means the core need on the inside of every human's heart to be loved unconditionally was created *by* God, *for* God, and *from* God.

God put within us a deep need for communion with Him because that's His deepest desire. That's why He made us. And so, if we're made in His likeness and His image, then we are compelled to love, just like God.

The First Exchange

Why is it that we don't experience life like this? We long to know the truth about how to access a life of fulfillment, but left to our human nature, we try to find that truth and power in ways that will never give life. The Apostle Paul tells us why:

> *For even though they knew God, they did not honor Him as God or give thanks, but they became futile in their speculations, and their foolish heart was darkened. Professing to be wise, they became fools, and exchanged the glory of the incorruptible God for an image in the form of corruptible man. . . . For they exchanged the truth of God for a lie, and worshiped and served the creature rather than the Creator, who is blessed forever. Amen.*
>
> —Rom. 1:21–23, 25

When God made Adam and Eve, they enjoyed a seamless intimacy with the God of the universe in the Garden of Eden.

However, Adam and Eve chose not to honor God and began to worship "the creature." Even though they knew God, they did not honor Him. They broke communion with Him. That's bizarre to imagine, isn't it? They were able to experience life with God face-to-face with no disruption, yet they stopped honoring Him as God when they began to listen to and yield to the Enemy. It says *they exchanged the truth of God for a lie*" (Rom. 1:25). This is all of mankind; before the truth of salvation is revealed to us, we are all worshipping and serving the creature, and we have all exchanged God's truth for a lie. We'll explore this more in the next chapter, but the point here is that mankind stopped honoring Him and became futile in their speculations.

What does futility mean? It means pointless or useless. When we depend on our way of thinking and our understanding of life apart from God, it's useless. These ways of thinking are rooted in humanity's limited understanding, called speculations. Our independence from God in the way we process and live our lives is useless because we cannot produce life-giving good apart from Him.

We are looking for truth—the truth about how to live a life of fullness. But apart from God, we define truth by our own experience, making up our own rules for how life should be lived. Living without connecting and yielding to who God is and what His ways are has no power since He's the One who created true life. Think about how many man-made solutions we come up with for man-made problems that only produce more problems. Living apart from God is useless—futile—and brings darkness to our hearts. I may be using strong language, but that is what the Word of God says.

When Adam and Eve chose not to honor God, they

actually made a choice to stop worshipping Him and began to worship themselves. The word *worship* doesn't just mean going to church on Sunday, singing some songs, and then checking the box that you've completed it. To worship something means to devote yourself to whatever has your attention and affection. To worship God means we abandon our own understanding, our own rules, and our own way of living and give Him our attention and affection, yielding to Him as the truth. This Exchange message is ultimately about making the choice to yield to God.

. . . .

To worship something means to devote yourself to whatever has your attention and affection.

. . . .

God is the only One worthy of our worship. He is the only Righteous One who created us and redeemed us because He loves us so. He created us to be in communion with Him, and through that communion, His beauty is expressed to a family He desires to share it with. He designed the way the world works according to His nature.

To not align with His design by giving ourselves to Him is foolishness since He made us in His image and knows what He designed us for. Fullness for us comes through receiving the Creator's purpose and living it in the highest way. It comes down to this: Who are you going to worship? Are you really going to worship God, or are you going to worship yourself, which ultimately is the Devil. Choosing to live independently from God is what the serpent convinced Eve to do, and Eve convinced Adam.

If I could boil down the entire gospel, it would come down to that. There's the Devil, and there's God. One deserves worship, and one does not but is always trying to get us to worship him. In the garden, Adam and Eve desired their own understanding to be elevated above God. The moment they decided that, they separated from God. That's what the Enemy wants to do to us all the time—to cause us to doubt God's goodness. If we allow that voice to lie to us about God, then we elevate our own understanding above trusting God, and we position ourselves *as* God. It is critical that we watch over our hearts. Worshipping (honoring, trusting) God keeps us rightly positioned to fulfill the call of God in our lives. That is the fear of the Lord.

The Power for Salvation

So where is the power for living a life of fulfillment? How do we restore the communion mankind once had with God? Let's look at what Romans 1:16–17 says: *"For I am not ashamed of the gospel, for it is the power of God for salvation to everyone who believes, to the Jew first and also to the Greek. For in it the righteousness of God is revealed from faith to faith; as it is written, 'BUT THE RIGHTEOUS MAN SHALL LIVE BY FAITH.'"*

. . . .

**God's redemption covers all your life
from beginning to end.**

. . . .

Paul tells us in this verse that he is not ashamed of the gospel because the good news of Christ is powerful to redeem what we lost. The power to access life that we have been seeking in our own understanding is found only in laying down everything to be with God. God's redemption of mankind and your personal salvation go so much further than just a one-time event that saves your soul from hell. As incredibly powerful as that is, God's redemption covers all your life from beginning to end. His redemptive power is enough to free you in every way, here and now, and to free you from the past as well.

REDEMPTION

The act of saving or being saved from sin, error, or evil; the act of regaining or gaining possession of something in exchange for payment, or clearing a debt.

Redemption is our ransom being paid in full; the total riddance, deliverance, and freedom from the bondage we were doomed to live in. Christ recovered ownership of us through His own sacrifice. He legally paid for our debt and purchased us back from the state of sin and consequences of sin. Any area of our life the accuser had access to devour, we now (through God's empowerment) can reclaim.

Salvation means a daily fullness of provision, power, healing, deliverance, and rich companionship with the Father, Son, and Holy Spirit. You've entered into a covenant relationship with God Himself. All that God is, is promised to us in salvation.

Before Paul's conversion, he believed he had the truth. He was a well-respected leader among the Jews. Paul is a guy who had everything going for him in the natural world (Phil. 3:5–6). Then, on the road to Damascus, he had an encounter with Jesus Christ. He knew he'd just been delivered from what he thought was life, but he had no power. It didn't bring the knowledge of God's love, which was life-changing. For Paul to say he is not ashamed of the gospel and that it's the good news that delivered him shows just how life-changing salvation was for Paul. He's not ashamed to have no power in himself to bring life or good, which was contrary to his former way of living when he tried to fulfill the Law. He admitted that only Christ has power to redeem and restore.

The first time I seriously sat down with Romans 1:16–17, I found it overwhelming because it was the answer to the foundational question I'd been asking since I was a teenager. *Where is the power?* That was the question that started my search for a deeper understanding. These verses in Romans provide the answer. *The power is in the gospel.*

The purpose of the gospel isn't just to save us from our sin but to restore life with God as He originally designed us to have it (John 14:6). The purpose is for us to *know* God. We want His righteousness to flow through us as we make choices every day. We are designed to always respond and relate to Him, to be dependent on His nature, His attributes, and His power. He loved us so much that He gave His own life so we could know Him and be with Him where He is (John 3:16).

It is in the gospel that God's goodness, character, faithfulness, and ability are revealed. The word *revealed* means the veil has been pulled back. When you meet God, the Spirit pulls back the veil of your understanding about life, and then revelation comes into your being.

That's what Paul meant when he referenced his encounter with God in his letter to the Corinthians. He said that when he met God on the road to Damascus, the veil was pulled off him. He said he was blind, but now he could see. Where he was dull, now he was alive (2 Cor. 3:12–18).

The fullness of the good news is this: truly knowing (gaining revelation of) God through His Word is what sets us free. If we are yielding to another voice already, believing lies instead of the truth of God, we will have a hard time accessing the goodness of God. If we're already full of ourselves and our own understanding, then there's no room for the fullness of God. We can't overcome this world if we don't have faith that God is with us and *for us* in our circumstances.

· · · · · · · · · · · · · · · ·

The fullness of the good news is this: truly knowing (gaining revelation of) God through His Word is what sets us free.

· · · · · · · · · · · · · · · ·

God, through Christ, made a way for us to be restored to His original purpose in creating mankind. He desires to have a family He can commune with. The highest and best life a person can have is to fulfill the purpose he or she was created for through worshipping the one true God. We were created to be known and loved to the fullest extent and to love the greatest One to our fullest capacity with no fear of shame. Christ made this possible!

We were made to glorify God. We cannot function apart from Him and expect life to come forth.

The Fullness of God

In Ephesians 3:17–19, Paul writes, "*[T]hat you, being rooted and grounded in love, may be able to comprehend with all the saints what is the breadth and length and height and depth, and to know the love of Christ which surpasses knowledge, that you may be filled up to all the fullness of God.*"

Paul also writes about this in Colossians 2:9–10: "*For in Him all the fullness of Deity dwells in bodily form, and in Him you have been made complete, and He is the head over all rule and authority.*" The fullness of God is in Christ. And if you have yielded to Christ the Savior, you become one with God through Christ. All of God is in Christ, who is in you, and our part is to yield to Christ within us.

The way we are filled up to all fullness is by knowing the love of Christ. This is the starting place. The transformation begins when we receive the love God is offering us. When we receive the love of God and our new position in Him, His fullness begins to fill us and spill out into our lives. Again, this isn't just a single transaction we make with God to receive His love. We receive His love in every circumstance for every issue, trusting Him to redeem us and meet our needs.

But this can't happen if we have accepted lies and are living according to our own ideas or agendas about how we think life should go. There won't be room for us to be filled up with Christ's love. We have to deal with those issues first.

Finding Fullness

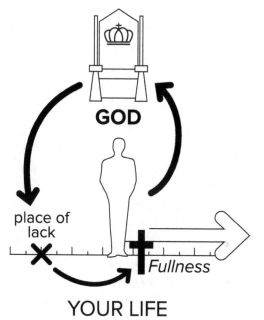

Fullness Diagram

So, how do you get filled up with the love and knowledge of Christ, exchanging your understanding for His? Sometimes it helps to see a picture of how this process works. Imagine the whole of your life on a timeline as shown in the Fullness Diagram. You've had all kinds of experiences and beliefs. An experience as simple as a rude or dismissive comment someone said to us in second grade can have a major influence on how our lives are shaped. Sometimes it's as intense as being sexually abused or orphaned or experiencing a traumatic death. God has something to say about all of it, no matter how big or small. We can call these experiences points of pain or places of lack (represented in the diagram with an *X*).

We build our beliefs around what happened to us in those experiences. Our beliefs are a mixture of our broken responses to our life's experiences and the systems around us—family values, the society we grew up in, authority figures who have influenced us. Your beliefs can also come from your personality, but remember, it's your fallen personality. The root of it is that I am going to do whatever it takes for me to be okay.

This belief that it is up to you is the root of our humanity without God. I'm going to do whatever I have to do to be okay, even if that means I have to punch you in the nose or elevate myself so I look like a good person, a person who wants to bless others and be seen as a good Christian. The motivation behind these actions is about getting what I think I need to be okay in life. This is coping—just making it through, trying to survive. The capacity for these coping strategies is in us from the time we're born, and the beliefs and behaviors develop over time.

Throughout our lives, we've stored within us thousands of experiences, often not knowing what's going to trigger something in us or how we'll cope. All along the way, we each have God's embedded blueprint of needing deep communion and intimacy with Him, so we start to feel frustrated, sad, hopeless, and lonely, bumping into our lack over and over. At some point, our coping stops benefiting us, and our triggers stop us from being able to move through life. We call that a "stuck place." Some people describe the feeling as hitting a wall in life.

Throughout this book, we will share real stories of people who have had breakthroughs because of the Exchange. Their names have been changed, but their personal revelations and transformations are real. Ben is one of those stories.

Ben was familiar with his "stuck place." Although he had been a born-again Christian for many years, he could never overcome feelings of deep and overwhelming rage. Certain circumstances in his life would bring up this rage, usually related to feeling unsuccessful or as though he couldn't make progress in life. Ben's rage was paralyzing, and he felt like a very real, invisible force was keeping a hand on him, holding him back from opportunities to advance in every area of his life. He truly felt stuck and was angry with himself, others around him, and God.

After learning about the Exchange process, Ben had a ministry session. The Lord took Ben back on his timeline and showed him a traumatic experience when he had chosen to believe a lie about himself.

When Ben was two years old, he was riding in the back seat of a two-door Chevy with his older sister. Their mother was dropping them off at preschool, and Ben was dressed in white slacks and a blue blazer for picture day. He was playing with the silver door lock on the passenger door when his mother leaned across the seat to open that door and let him out. Ben lost his balance and fell from the car to the pavement. In her panic, his mother reached for him, but when she did, her foot came off the brake, and the car ran over Ben's little body.

During the ministry session, Ben described his experience like this:

> I saw the whole incident play out as though I were watching a movie. I was immediately filled with fear and pain about my life and my future—in the memory I felt

stuck. The Lord revealed to me that as a two-year-old boy, I felt like no one was going to take care of me, so I believed I had to take care of myself. Throughout my life, I saw I was completely incapable of this task—taking care of myself by myself—and as a result, I felt afraid and incredibly angry. These were the same confusing thoughts and feelings I experienced anytime an opportunity for advancement came in my life, whether in sports, business, or meaningful relationships.

Ben lived with this lie from that point onward, and it was like a black thread in a white tapestry, tainting all of his experiences.

Exchanging the Truth for Lies

Our current "stuck places" are rooted in a lie that we believed when we experienced a painful place of lack. How do I know that? Go back to Romans 1:25. *"For they exchanged the truth of God for a lie, and worshiped and served the creature rather than the Creator."* It was this verse that awakened in me the idea of the Exchange ministry. The key to the Exchange is this: wherever there is a lack of revelation in me to understand the goodness and righteousness of God, it is because I believe a lie.

. . . .

Wherever there is a lack of revelation in me to understand the goodness and righteousness of God, it is because I believe a lie.

. . . .

It's that simple. Wherever you're stuck, it's because you believe a lie somewhere. You were not able to apprehend or acknowledge the goodness of God; you were unable to honor Him and choose to worship Him in a painful past experience. Then you believed a lie about God, about the world, or about yourself—or maybe all three. That caused you not to know God in that place. The lie is taking up space inside of you instead of God taking up that space.

When we experience physical pain, our immediate reaction is to stop the pain. If we have a headache, we take ibuprofen. When we experience emotional pain, however, our first reaction is not usually to dig deep and find out what's really going on so we can help the emotional pain. Until we learn how to do that, our emotional pains will result in the acceptance of our own understanding, which is usually embedded in lies.

Sometimes we realize we're stuck because we made a judgment about who God is based on past experience. We decided who God is because of something an authority figure did that wounded us or because of some false expectation about how God should be. We didn't know how to access Him as the truth, and we made a judgment about His character. Often we aren't even aware that we're doing it. It isn't because He wasn't really there or He didn't do anything. It's because we didn't know Him for who He truly is, and we didn't know how to tap into what He was doing.

For example, we might say, "If God is just, He wouldn't have allowed my sister to be robbed." Or we might say, "If God is good, surely He'll provide [this specific way] for me." These are examples of us defining God who sees and knows all things by our own understanding, which is based on limited knowledge of the full situation. It also excludes free will in humans and their choices that affect people's lives. We will discuss that more in depth in Chapter 6.

It would be nice to believe that at the moment of salvation we all get a clean slate and start over—that all those stored experiences would just go away. But that doesn't happen. Instead, what we have is the knowledge of the love of God, the security of God, and the power of God so we can overcome. We were born into a universe where sin rules over us. We've had life experiences that have been hurtful and wounding. And now Christ comes in, and God wants to redeem those painful places to train us to be overcomers. That is how we learn His nature and ways so we can subdue the earth in His likeness, which is what He commissioned us to do in Genesis 1:26–28.

You might be thinking, *Okay, I've got baggage, but I have Jesus.* True, but you're walking, and you keep hitting a wall. I imagine a situation has already come to mind that you continue running into, a wall you just keep hitting. By now, God is beginning to touch something within you that you haven't been able to resolve yourself—a place where you're stuck. It could be broken relationships. It could be financial issues. It could be rejection or a fear of trusting people. Maybe you feel that circumstances never work out for you. But the Bible says it's the kindness of God that leads you to repentance, that makes you turn around (Rom. 2:4).

These walls are God's kindness to you. That may be hard to believe now, but hopefully by the end of this book, you will believe it. It doesn't feel good to hit a wall—people rejecting us, financial difficulties, inferior feelings. None of these things feel good. But there's another way to look at them. Walls are there to get you fed up with what the Enemy stole from you so you will shift your perspective and access the presence of Jesus within you. He's been with you each time you got stuck or hit the wall. Now He can send the Holy Spirit to show you where you're stuck and redeem it.

The Lord can come in and set right anything that has become horribly skewed. The Exchanged life is about learning how to commune with God, go deep into your spirit to connect with what He did for you, and learn how to be His son or daughter at every juncture of life.

Making the Exchange

The One who made us is the only One who is able to complete what He began in us. He is the only One who can restore what we lost through our independence from His original desire to have a deep, abiding relationship with us. He can do this because God has always been and always will be. He is infinite, outside of time and space. He is in our past, present, and future. He is a present God, always waiting for us to include Him in our journey.

He is not bound by time, so He is able to go back into our life experiences and reveal to us how they have impacted us. When He shows us the lies we have believed and the trauma we have faced, He always shows us His heart and truth in those situations as well.

Remember, God is redemptive. His heart toward us is always beneficent. He desires to take back every ounce of life the Enemy stole from us and restore us to a deep and unbroken communion with Him. That means there is nothing, truly nothing, in your life that is outside of His power to redeem and restore.

. . . .

That means there is nothing, truly nothing, in your life that is outside of His power to redeem and restore.

. . . .

God is infinite and redemptive, and He has a redeeming plan for every moment of your life. Bring your "stuck place" and your pain to God, and ask Him these two questions:

1. God, what is this?

2. What do I do with it?

These two questions can help redirect how you react to situations or help you process a painful place in your past. Go back to the Fullness Diagram. These questions are how we go up (see the arrow pointing up) or look first to the Lord to help us when we feel stuck.

Remember, it's all about who you worship. If it's the Lord, then you want every place and every thought to be occupied by Him. Second Corinthians 10:5 says, *"We are destroying speculations and every lofty thing raised up against the knowledge of God, and we are taking every thought captive to the obedience of Christ."* Asking these two questions of the Lord helps you hear from God's truth and perspective in the moment instead of trying to figure it out on your own, living separately from Him. Taking your thoughts captive to the obedience of Christ is an act of worship. Anytime we take our eyes off Him and look at things around us, we disconnect ourselves from our place of relationship with Him, shifting our identity from faith in God to faith in something else.

Because God is the infinite One, He knows what you believed in those moments of pain. If the Lord takes you back on your timeline to a painful memory, ask Him, "God, where were You in that situation, and what do You want to say about it?" Ask Him what lies you believed. God knows you intimately. If the problem is that you believed a lie, He knows all the lies you believed and what moment(s) caused the "stuck place." He can show you what you believed, when you started believing it, and why you believed it. You want the Lord to identify the places where you've believed lies because it's part of the redeeming process. He's the only One who can show us with His redemptive power.

God in His wonder-working power will take you back on your timeline (the arrows pointing back to the place of lack). After showing you the condition of your heart and the lies you agreed with, He will reveal His truth to you. He will tell you the truth of that experience, and you can literally exchange the lie for the truth. Then you can begin to believe what God has wanted to say to you. When that happens, a thread of unbelief gets pulled out from your heart.

For Ben, God showed him the painful experience where he chose to believe a lie, and then He showed him what happened from heaven's perspective. After Ben asked, "Lord, where were You in that situation?" he immediately saw an angel holding up the back of the car, keeping it from crushing his small body. Ben also saw an angel of the Lord on the fire escape of the three-story school building. He was blowing a trumpet and declaring the calling of his life over him and the situation.

When Ben's mother rushed him to the hospital, the doctor

was amazed at what he saw. Ben had a broken arm from the fall out of the car, but even with the evidence of tire tracks on his white slacks and blue blazer, he was miraculously unscathed. In that moment, the Lord had saved him from being crushed by the weight of the car, and now the Lord was redeeming Ben's heart from being under the weight of the Enemy's lie all those years.

When we ask Him, God always shows up with an incredible, life-changing truth about His heart toward us. In that moment, we experience God's love for us in a very personal way, and we can make an exchange. Remember how I said that the way we are filled up to all the fullness is by knowing the love of Christ? This is what I meant. Knowing His love in our most painful experiences is what unlocks our hearts and reveals truth. We can then engage it with our faith and say:

"Lord, I repent for believing the lie(s) that _____."

"Lord, I now accept Your truth that _____."

Let me talk about the power of this moment in the Exchange. You can say mantras over yourself all day long that you are loved, worthy, and equipped. You can have friends and family speak truth over you for years. You can try to input things from the outside to change how you think, but they will not have the same immediate, transformational power that happens when the Holy Spirit of God reveals the truth to you. It is only by His divine touch, His divine revelation, and His divine love that you can truly be transformed. He is the only One who can reveal the lie that's taking the place of His truth in your heart. Everything else we try is self-effort and coping.

You may have forty threads, but each one you deal with is woven through all your history. Once a lie is removed, it changes your perspective about what happened to you. Then every other time that lie weaves into your perception, God can show you what His intention was and how He sees you in a redemptive way. He shows you who you've been from the foundation of the world.

Now you can put away those childish things, as Paul tells us in 1 Corinthians 13. You believed those lies when you were young—lies that you weren't loved or were alone or whatever you agreed with the Enemy about. You can put that away now and come into maturity. You can take hold of what God says about you, how He sees you, and exchange the one for the other. When that happens, a thread of unbelief that has shaped the way you have seen things throughout your life is pulled out. The fullness of God now has a place within you to reside.

In Ben's life, the lie that he would have to take care of himself was replaced with a golden strand of truth. God showed Ben that He was there and had been taking care of him all along. Ben experienced an encounter with the Lord that changed his heart, changed his mind, and showed him how and why he was made. He shifted from just petitioning the Lord about his anger to an everlasting pursuit of oneness.

Ben took biblical action by forgiving his mother and repenting for his agreement with the lie, and he was liberated. He said, "I feel freer than ever before, and I now experience a new ability to approach opportunities without confusion and feeling held back. Now I trust the Lord to be with me and take care of me the way I've needed Him to all along."

Ben's redemption was tied to his destiny. The Enemy tried to steal his future. God not only had an angel rescue Ben but also sent another angel to trumpet out the purpose of Ben's life.

This is what we're after. Once the Lord does the redeeming work in you, your current "stuck place" or wall is dealt with, and a part of your destiny is unlocked. Often the "stuck place" completely dissolves, but if any residue remains, you can access the resurrection power of Christ to overcome the wall through exercising your faith. Now you can move forward on your timeline of life where once you were blocked.

Every person can live a life like this all the time. You won't always have to go to someone else to find out why you're stuck. Eventually, you'll be able to do this and have enough faith that God is going to tell you His truths because His sheep hear His voice (John 10:27). You can hear His voice. You can ask Him anything, and He hears you. He'll reveal what He wants you to know according to His will and in His timing because He's an extravagantly good God.

Hearing God

We talk a lot in this book about asking God, listening to God, and hearing from God. It is impossible to live an Exchanged life without hearing from God. It is a very significant piece to our walk with God, but it's truly simple. We can talk back and forth with God just like we do in human relationships. If we can't hear what someone else is saying or means, how can that relationship come into unity and flourish?

In John 10, the Lord takes a whole chapter to talk about

His voice in relation to His children. He talks about His character and the how and why of His children being able to trust His voice. When you begin to know who God is, you will discern His voice more easily. You will know the difference between His voice, the Enemy's voice, and your own voice.

To make it simple, let me give you a quick way to discern each of those. God's voice is kind and not pushy, it's peaceful, it builds up and doesn't condemn, and it produces hope even in correction. The Enemy's voice is demanding, accusing, and agitating. Your voice is bent toward self. The main character is you.

As you live an Exchanged life, it's important to learn to identify these three voices because who you listen to is who you yield to or worship. When you are processing your life situations, ask the Lord questions about how you got stuck, what impacted you, and who was involved. Learning to dialogue with God all the way through your situations and emotions is critical to knowing how to work through the healing process.

The Exchange message takes the foundational truths of the gospel, which I'll explain in the coming chapters, and shows the practical application of them for your everyday life. While it is a clear desire of most Christians to live a good life, we often find that accessing a life of fullness is a difficult or impossible feat to do on our own. The gospel message was not sent to teach us how to be good; the gospel is the *power* of God to *transform* us. As you read about the gospel on these pages, surrender to the process of transformation as well. You now have the tools to engage God's heart in ways you've likely never heard before.

. . . .

The gospel message was not sent to teach us how to be good; the gospel is the *power* of God to *transform* us.

. . . .

In this chapter, we've covered a lot of material. We discussed God's intention to have deep communion with us and mankind's desire for independence, which broke the communion we shared. Our disobedience didn't stop God from loving us. He still desires communion with us, and He made us to have the same desire. Though we disobeyed, God never left us. As a matter of fact, God's love is chasing us down, chasing you down, so He can have a relationship with us all. God sent His Son to repair the breach in our relationship with Him.

The gospel contains the power of salvation. Our salvation lies in knowing God and living our lives in communion with Him. When we do this, our lives overflow with the fullness of God, which spreads to others. When we exchange lies for the truth and build our faith in that truth, we get unstuck and can begin to live a life in the freedom God intended. By living this way, we can live a life of fullness.

Personal Processing

Meditate on These Verses

For I am not ashamed of the gospel, for it is the power of God for salvation to everyone who believes, to the Jew first and also to the Greek. For in it the righteousness of God is revealed from faith to faith; as it is written, "BUT THE RIGHTEOUS MAN SHALL LIVE BY FAITH."

—Rom. 1:16–17

[A]nd that you, being rooted and grounded in love, may be able to comprehend with all the saints what is the breadth and length and height and depth, and to know the love of Christ which surpasses knowledge, that you may be filled up to all the fullness of God.

—Eph. 3:17–19

For even though they knew God, they did not honor Him as God or give thanks, but they became futile in their speculations, and their foolish heart was darkened. Professing to be wise, they became fools, and exchanged the glory of the incorruptible God for an image in the form of corruptible man and of birds and four-footed animals and crawling creatures.

Therefore God gave them over in the lusts of their hearts to impurity, so that their bodies would be dishonored among them. For they exchanged the truth of God for a lie, and worshiped and served the creature rather than the Creator, who is blessed forever. Amen.

—Rom. 1:21–25

Read Deuteronomy 8:1–5 and Judges 3:1–5.

Dialogue with the Lord about the following questions (write down your answers because the Lord may want to speak to you more about them):

1. What have you always thought was the main purpose of salvation? After reading this chapter, has your answer changed?

2. Where are you currently hitting a wall in your life? Where have you felt stuck before?

Don't feel pressure to go through the full Exchange process yet unless the Lord leads you to. Remember, you're only in the first chapter. Take time this week to observe yourself and see where you might be experiencing a "stuck place."

Prayer

"So faith comes from hearing, and hearing by the word of Christ" (Rom. 10:17). *Declare this prayer out loud:*

Lord Jesus, I confess You are the only true source of life and truth. I want to comprehend Your love and be filled up to all Your fullness like it says in Ephesians. I lay down all my ways of protecting myself, controlling my life, and gaining false fulfillment, and I say yes to Your invitation to journey with You. I will go with You wherever You lead. Amen.

Chapter 2

BLAME AND SHAME

For even though they knew God, they did not honor Him as God or give thanks, but they became futile in their speculations, and their foolish heart was darkened. Professing to be wise, they became fools, and exchanged the glory of the incorruptible God for an image in the form of corruptible man.

—Rom. 1:21–23

In the last chapter, we mentioned that God created us to be in intimate communion with Him, but because of disobedience, we now live in a broken world. To truly understand how great the divide is between mankind's ways and God's ways, we are going to take a deeper look at what happened in the Garden of Eden with Adam and Eve.

When Adam and Eve chose independence from God, they began to fill their places of shame with self-life. They relied on human reasoning and coping mechanisms that further separated mankind from the Lord and from one another.

We have a lot of evidence that shows that when left to themselves, humans are incapable of producing what is necessary for totally successful, purposeful, and fulfilling relationships. Each of us has a desire to find completeness and contentment in the deepest places within us. But without God, we lack the ability to achieve what we so long for—communion to the fullest measure. Only God can fill us up and make us whole again.

Let Them Rule over the Planet

God created mankind in His image to bring His glory to the earth. In Genesis 1:26–28, God gave the planet to mankind to fill and subdue it. This was one of the ways God intended mankind to reflect Him.

God created the planet for us, and as our Father, He told us to rule (manage, give order to, bring into alignment). Don't parents do the same thing? They entrust things to their children. You may tell your kids, "Now go subdue your bedroom, please." (I'm sure you don't say it that way; probably more like, "Take care of that mess!") That doesn't mean they always do it well, but it is the task they have responsibility over.

Just as a parent trains their children to carry out their responsibilities, God wants to work with us. A child learns the ways of the parents by being trained by them. God didn't intend for us to rule and subdue independent of Him. Remember, He made us for relationship. God was available to Adam and Eve in a literal way. He walked with them in the cool of the day, having a deep relationship in all things.

The Garden of Eden wasn't a bubble that God created for Adam and Eve. He meant for them to fill it and then subdue it. I want to quickly talk about the word *subdue* because that word can feel negative. The connotation of *subdue* is forcing something or being overpowered. Maybe someone has tried to subdue your identity. The word *subdue* actually means to bring into order. God was telling Adam and Eve to order the earth. We have rule over our circumstances; they don't have rule over us.

Keep in mind that God told Adam and Eve to rule and subdue the earth when they were still living in complete communion with Him, abiding in His character and ways. His original intent was for us to live dependent on Him. It was our independence that created the breach.

. . . .

**His original intent was for us
to live dependent on Him.
It was our independence
that created the breach.**

. . . .

When God created us, He gave us free will. He desires to be in a relationship with us, and that same desire is written in our hearts. But when we consider the nature of love, we must acknowledge that it is a choice. God doesn't force Himself on us. Forced love isn't love. He isn't a micromanager or a puppeteer. He is always inviting us into a relationship with

Him. He says, "Here's fullness. Will you respond to me? Will you come and draw into me?"

He invites, and we respond with a choice. Pay attention to how Adam and Eve used their free will and responsibility to rule as we look at the story of the Fall.

Fall from Glory

Before the Fall, Adam and Eve lived in communion with God, radiating His image and nature. Genesis 2:25 tells us, *"And the man and his wife were both naked and were not ashamed."* That doesn't mean they were just comfortable with their bodies without clothes. It means they weren't self-aware or self-focused. They had no idea they were created with need or lack and, therefore, weren't worried about their need to be dependent. They weren't lack-conscious but rather God-conscious.

Imagine what that was like—never worrying if you said something wrong or didn't measure up in some way. You were just living freely, knowing God thinks you are amazing and will meet all your needs. This lack of awareness was how God made us—to live in His image and nature in total communion with Him 24/7, totally secure.

Read what happened next in Genesis 3:1–13:

Now the serpent was more crafty than any beast of the field which the LORD GOD had made. And he said to the woman, "Indeed, has God said, 'You shall not eat from any tree of the garden'?" The woman said to the serpent, "From the fruit of the trees of the garden we may eat; but from the fruit of the tree which is in the middle of the garden, God has said, 'You shall not eat from it or touch it, or you will die.'" The serpent said to the woman, "You surely will not die! For God knows that in the day you eat from it your eyes will be opened, and you will be like God, knowing good and evil." When the woman saw that the tree was good for food, and that it was a delight to the eyes, and that the tree was desirable to make one wise, she took from its fruit and ate; and she gave also to her husband with her, and he ate. Then the eyes of both of them were opened, and they knew that they were naked; and they sewed fig leaves together and made themselves loin coverings.

They heard the sound of the LORD GOD walking in the garden in the cool of the day, and the man and his wife hid themselves from the presence of the LORD GOD among the trees of the garden. Then the LORD GOD called to the man, and said to him, "Where are you?" He said, "I heard the sound of You in the garden, and I was afraid because I was naked; so I hid myself." And He said, "Who told you that you were naked? Have you eaten from the tree of which I commanded you not to eat?" The man said, "The woman whom You gave to be with me, she gave me from the tree, and I ate." Then the LORD GOD said to the woman, "What is this you have done?" And the woman said, "The serpent deceived me, and I ate."

Adam and Eve began entertaining a different voice—the serpent. He convinced them that they would not die if they ate from the Tree of the Knowledge of Good and Evil, as God had told them. The serpent told the woman, *"You surely will not die! For God knows that on the day you eat from it your eyes will be opened, and you will be like God, knowing good and evil"* (Gen 3:4–5). Satan was tempting them to think they could be like God apart from God, which was exactly what Lucifer (Satan) did that got him kicked out of heaven. He wanted all the worship for himself.

Here the deception begins. Having evil present in our lives or around us is not the problem. The problem is when we begin to entertain another voice. As believers, when we stop yielding to the Father's voice, we will yield to another. We do it many times without even being aware of it.

You may already be thinking, *That's not me. I know the Bible and have studied it my whole life. I know how to discern what comes from the world and what comes from God.* That may certainly be true. You may be surprised, though, that some of your beliefs may *sound* like they come from God, but it is God according to our humanity; it is God's truth without revelation from Him about what He means or what it means for us in our lives.

Let me give you an example. When someone has an offense against us, such as maligning our character, we get offended. We feel justified in our anger because it truly was wrong, so we build our defense case with our justifications for why they should come to us and ask for forgiveness—because that is what the Bible says. But in the Word, God says, *"Be kind to one another, tender-hearted, forgiving each other, just as God in Christ also has forgiven you"* (Eph. 4:32). We need to take our hearts and our emotions to God and ask Him what His response is. We base our forgiveness on the other person's merit; God bases His forgiveness of us on His mercy.

. . . .

We base our forgiveness on the other person's merit; God bases His forgiveness of us on His mercy.

. . . .

God in His redemptive kindness understands that we will yield to voices other than His. One of my favorite verses is this: *"He is mindful that we are but dust"* (Ps. 103:14). He understands what has happened. He knows that before we are even able to process our life as a child, much less repent of our sin and come into agreement with Christ's truth, we already believed a lot of things from the Enemy. Why? Because we were born into a fallen world with a nature that's independent from God.

I don't believe this was the first time Adam and Eve had seen the serpent. It's the same with us. The Enemy doesn't just show up one day and tell us some horrific lie. He's been whispering lies to us little by little since the day we were born.

Genesis 3:6 says, *"When the woman saw that the tree was good for food."* Let's stop there for a moment. How did she know the tree was good for food? Did she ask the Lord if it was good for food? No. She decided that. She saw and decided. I'm laying this out so you see how we get duped. The serpent is cunning. In Genesis 3:4, the serpent said to the woman, *"You surely will not die!"* The serpent is making God out to be a liar and someone Eve can't trust. Look at the progression of Eve's process in Genesis 3:6: (1) she saw, (2) she thought it looked good, (3) she decided it would make her wise, and (4) she ate it. She did all this without communing with God.

She swallowed the lie the Enemy told her and with it, her own reasoning. Every time we make a decision without yielding to God and knowing what He says, we are agreeing with our own understanding. At its core, it is an antichrist spirit. The irony is that Adam and Eve were already like God, being made in His image, but they were tempted to be like Him *without* Him. We have the same issue. We think we should be like Him without thinking we need Him.

Blame and Shame

When Eve took the fruit and ate it and then gave some to Adam to eat, their eyes were opened, and they suddenly realized they were naked. Their eyes were opened to their dependent nature—God's design—and saw that making decisions apart from God does not make them like God. They were not complete, not the source of life, not holy apart from God. The knowledge of good and evil opens the door to measuring and weighing ourselves, others, and our circumstances apart from God. In Adam and Eve's own understanding, they felt deep shame. Because of their choice, this is the condition we are all born into. We do not have the capacity to bring life, perfection, or wholeness without God, and our inability brings us shame when we are not connected to Him.

Have you ever gotten into a conversation with someone and then insist on a stack of Bibles that your perspective is right? They insist on a stack of Bibles that theirs is right. We're sure that the way we think and see something is the right way. Our eyes are open, but they're open to the knowledge of good and evil, right and wrong, apart from God, and that's death. Adam and Eve fell from glory by choosing the knowledge of good and evil over life with God, and they became self-aware, independent from God, without hope, and with much fear and shame.

That moment must have been horrifying for them. They'd been clothed in God's glory, which was all they'd ever known. Then suddenly, they realized, "This is who I am apart from God."

Next, we read they heard the sound of the Lord walking in the garden, knew the gravity of what they'd just done, and hid themselves from His presence. It is amazing that even in their sin, they could still hear God. It's because of His mercy that He still allows us to hear Him, even in our sin.

Adam and Eve were hiding among some trees. Are we really any different? We have coping mechanisms to make ourselves feel better when really what we're doing is trying to cover our shame and self-awareness. We may not literally run and hide, but in many ways, we are hiding when we self-medicate with excessive use of food, alcohol, social media, sleep, and more. We are avoiding an honest look at ourselves. We are avoiding the consequences of our actions. But more than that, we are avoiding being seen by God. The more we can tear down these coping patterns and pull out the lies, the more the righteousness and fullness of God can come and fill us up.

When we live only unto God without self-consciousness, we're totally oblivious to our lack. Somebody might actually have to come and tell you, "Hey, the way you were acting a while ago did this to me." You might not be aware of it, and it's okay if that happens. Instead of having shame and feeling threatened by their statement, you'll be free to respond kindly because you're not trying to be everything by yourself. You're trusting in the righteousness of God. You can admit to that person, "Oh, I'm so sorry I affected you that way. I didn't mean to do that."

This is freedom.

In Genesis 3:9, God called for Adam and Eve. He wasn't asking because He didn't know where they were. He's always pursuing us in kindness—not to reprimand. Even in our sin, we can still hear Him calling for us. "Hey, where are you?" In other words, "Come on out. I'm right here. It's safe."

Adam responded, *"I heard the sound of You in the garden, and I was afraid because I was naked; so I hid myself"* (Gen. 3:10). God wanted to know who told them they were naked and then asked, *"Have you eaten from the tree of which I commanded you not to eat?"* (Gen. 3:11) (as if He didn't know). Adam said, *"The woman whom You gave to be with me, she gave me from the tree, and I ate"* (Gen. 3:12). The Lord asked Eve, *"What is this you have done?"* (Gen. 3:13).

Eve told God, *"The serpent deceived me, and I ate"* (Gen. 3:13). The Lord is gently pursuing them to come into confession because the sooner they do, the sooner they can have restoration. Pay attention to what Adam and Eve both reverted to. Shame naturally leads to not wanting to take responsibility for our own choices and instead blame it on each other or spiritual warfare. When you live life separated from your worth in God, your soul must somehow try to settle it in your conscience.

Some Christians love to blame things on the Devil. I believe in warfare, don't get me wrong, but I believe sometimes we experience warfare when there has been an open door through unbelief in God's ways either personally, in the atmosphere, or in those around us. As a believer, I'm still responsible to respond rightly to that warfare, whether it's in me or around me, because I have access to God and

His authority over the Enemy. We'll talk more about this in Chapter 6.

Adam and Eve felt shame because what they lacked was now preeminent in their minds. All they were aware of was what they lacked and how they were going to fix it. Adam and Eve were created to subdue the earth, but they gave their power of choice to the Enemy. They did not fulfill their assignment to rule the earth when they chose to listen to Satan. They gave him power through their agreement. The shame of their actions caused them to blame others and not take responsibility for their God-given free will.

Worship

Choosing to live independently from God is what Adam and Eve did. They turned their worship from God to their own understanding and therefore to the Enemy. In Chapter 1, we mentioned the war over worship. Some may have you believe the battle is against communism or Islam or secularism. The truth is, the war is between what Satan believes and what God believes, and consequently who we agree with (or worship).

You can reset your focus—your worship—on God at any moment because it's not based on your performance but on your faith in Him. If Adam and Eve would have stopped mid-decision about whether or not to eat the fruit and instead turned back to engaging God, reminding themselves of who He is, they could have shifted back to their true identity and chosen differently.

Notice, too, how the message between Eve and the serpent got twisted. Eve told the serpent they were not even allowed to touch the tree. But if we look at God's original conversation with Adam and Eve (Gen. 2:15–17), He doesn't mention anything about touching the tree. He wasn't trying to micromanage them with rules. He was protecting the relationship they had with Him and with each other. But in an effort to justify herself, Eve began creating parameters that God never set.

. . . .

**But in an effort to justify herself,
Eve began creating parameters that
God never set.**

. . . .

In our own lives, we try to respond based on what we think God wants, but that can mean we're withdrawing from a relationship with Him to uphold value systems He never asked for. An example is the virtue of loyalty. We know that God wants us to love one another and that having integrity and loyalty is one way to express that love. However, holding loyalty as the highest value can lead us to not set boundaries when we need to, or it can even keep us from making a move in obedience to God that might appear disloyal (such as changing jobs). We have to know what God is directing us to do in that area of our lives, not just what we've held as a high value.

Viewed this way, it makes sense how these little separations happen, particularly with Eve in this situation. A darkened understanding leads to separation from God.

Balancing Our Scales

Living under blame and shame begins a cycle of measuring ourselves against others, trying to cover up what we lack with coping mechanisms and blaming others when we fall short of expectations. We blame our parents, our spouses, and God; we even blame ourselves. We were born into a fallen world, living under the law of sin and death. When we operate separately from God's wisdom, the veil covers us and darkens our understanding.

Measuring is the way of the world. Everyone and everything operates under the knowledge of good and evil—right and wrong, good and bad. Have you ever walked into a room and someone ignores you? You automatically start trying to figure out if you've done something to offend them. You begin wondering if you were rude to that person in a previous interaction. Did you forget to do something you said you would do? You might even get defensive and think, *What's their problem?* We second-guess others' behaviors and try to reason through the situation because we are self-oriented. We start justifying ourselves and defend how we were right, innocent, or victimized.

We're concerned about being right and covering up what's wrong because of the Fall. Living in our own understanding and independent from God, whom we were designed to worship, is sin. Sin is choosing to gaze upon (to worship, to yield to) someone other than God. Our independence from God brings us both spiritual death and physical death.

. . . .

Sin is choosing to gaze upon (to worship, to yield to) someone other than God.

. . . .

Look at the scales in the Blame and Shame Diagram. The weight has to be balanced, the same on each side. If the scale isn't balanced, we add weight to the other side to balance it out. Blame and shame work that way. If I feel shame, then my scales are not balanced inside of me. I'm not okay. I'm going to do what it takes to get my scales balanced no matter what. The most natural way to achieve this is by using blame.

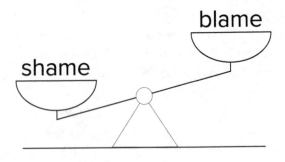

Blame and Shame Diagram

I'll give an example about what happens in traffic when someone cuts me off. Something happens that I don't expect and don't have control over. Most people respond in anger and blame. *That person was so rude! It's their fault I'm going to be late now. How dare they take advantage of me! It's because of them that I have all these negative feelings.*

It's true that someone's choices can have a negative impact on me, but underneath all that anger is a feeling of fear and an offense that life didn't go my way. Now my conscience is pricked because in my heart I responded critically to that person. To cover over my shame, I blame them for my resentment. I don't want to have responsibility over my own reactions. I'd rather blame them so I feel better in my conscience about fuming over them.

Rhiannon knew how it felt to be weighed down by measuring. She'd spent most of her life without her father. He left when she was young, and she carried the hurt from that abandonment with her from that point on. That abandonment caused pain in her life, revealing that she couldn't fill that hole on her own. Even as a young girl, Rhiannon felt ashamed that her father had left her, and the Enemy spoke a loud and clear message to her through her father's abandonment: *You're tainted. You're not pretty enough. You're not valuable enough. You don't deserve a prosperous future; you don't have a future. Your father's abandonment was the final word on where your life is going— nowhere.*

She believed it, blaming herself for his abandonment and blaming herself for feeling pain. The Enemy's lies became reality to her, and she constantly felt the weight and shame of living under that impossible measurement. She lived in fear, hopelessness, anger, relational strife, and deep heart pain that fueled disbelief and distrust about God's goodness toward her or in having a prosperous future.

As an adult, she experienced conflict in her marriage and felt held back from her dreams. All marriages experience conflict, but for Rhiannon, the pain and emotions were overwhelming. She responded to marital conflicts by self-blaming, feeling crushed at the most minor conflict because it confirmed her feelings of worthlessness. She immediately felt a familiar sting that would overload her emotions, making it difficult to process interpersonally or communicate her feelings. At the same time, she had deep feelings of insecurity when doing course work that she knew would give her a more prosperous future. Rhiannon could not stop feeling valueless and not enough.

We're always trying to balance this internal scale. We walk around imbalanced, and our neighbor walks around doing the same thing. Back and forth we're bumping into each other trying to balance the scales so we feel okay. Imagine if everyone we interacted with functioned like this, balancing the scales with shame and blame. It happens every day.

Measurement is the response we have from living under the Old Testament Law. We want people to see us as good or worthy. We'll do whatever we need to do so the other person doesn't think a mistake was our fault or so they don't feel the effects of our imperfection. There are many ways we measure ourselves according to our lack. Sometimes it's not even that someone else is doing the measuring. When we respond to life by measuring, we project that feeling to those around us. We make room for others to then measure us. The other person may not even be measuring us, but because we're so aware of our lack and the shame of it, we put off signals that we think we're being measured because we're actually measuring ourselves. That attracts measurement. Measuring ourselves in this way isn't a biblical mind-set. John 3:34 says, *"He gives the Spirit without measure."* When I believe and think about the fullness of the Spirit in me without measure, I will not be a person who is always measuring myself or others. Remember, we were designed with lack and will never measure up. We are to be filled up with Christ.

. . . .

When I believe and think about the fullness of the Spirit in me without measure, I will not be a person who is always measuring myself or others.

. . . .

The truth is that what is lacking in me can probably be filled up by the people around me. If I'm not so concerned about what I lack and what that says about me, then I'm happy for others to fill in my insufficiencies. But if I'm trying to be complete within myself, lacking nothing, then I don't want you to fill up something lacking in me because I want to be all of it myself.

Your former self may be warring with this notion. Within our deepest selves, we want recognition instead of being secure in who we are because of Christ, whether we are seen or not. We aren't in the habit of making room for others. We want our value to come through what we can add to life instead of knowing we have value whether others deem us valuable or not (or valuable by our own ways of measuring value). We're jealous and envious because we have these bent mentalities that started with the serpent (Isa. 14:12–15).

Not only is the pressure to measure built into our fallen nature, but the Law pressures us as well to measure up to an impossible standard.

The Letter of the Law

In the Old Covenant, the Law was God's way of teaching His chosen people. Galatians 3:23 tells us, *"But before faith came," we were kept in custody under the law, being shut up to the faith which was later to be revealed."*

The Law, the pressure we feel to be perfect or great apart from God, became the guide to lead us to Christ so we would become justified by faith. The Law causes us to have a constant preoccupation with measuring our sins. That includes feeling worthless because we sinned or feeling good because we didn't sin. Sin-consciousness is a constant preoccupation with sin, a product of living under the knowledge of good and evil. It's a vague and pervasive feeling that we sinned, that we are about to sin, or that someone else is about to sin. Sin-consciousness says our worth is based on whether or not we have sinned.

When Paul heard God's voice on the road to Damascus, he had a revelation. As we discussed in the previous chapter, Paul followed the Jewish Law with exactitude. He persecuted and killed Christians because of Christians' radical teachings about the one true God. Paul thought he knew the right way to live. He was living under the Law, a right-wrong value system.

When Paul (called Saul at the time) encountered Jesus and Jesus asked him, *"Saul, Saul, why are you persecuting Me?"* (Acts 9:4), the veil was removed because he met the Lord and believed. He saw the broken system he was living in. He realized that all his intelligence and all his law-abiding were of no worth. Later, in his letter to the church at Rome, Paul wrote that he is not ashamed of the gospel. He was transformed and delivered from a religious life of death to a yielded life in God.

Because of the cross, the One who was perfect and blameless absolutely gave Himself in our place to make us just. Justification means more than just the forgiveness of sin. When Jesus, the only Righteous One, shed His blood for us, we don't just get to skip over the consequences of our sin. His blood removes it entirely. Imagine a bank account that is deeply in the negative. God not only paid to bring the account back into the black, but He gave us endless capital by placing His Son in our spirit, giving us a brand-new nature at our core—a complete victory over our sin nature.

In our innermost being, we are restored to a sinless state like Adam and Eve before the Fall. Justification frees us from needing to meet the Law's expectations, our own expectations, or another's expectations. When we live by any standard other than God's, it becomes our idol. But we are only bound to live as God's sons and daughters through faith in Christ.

Our salvation is not based on measuring rights and wrongs. Under the new law, the new covenant of Jesus Christ, we are sons and daughters of God. When God looks at us, He sees His Son.

[F]or all have sinned and fall short of the glory of God, being justified as a gift by His grace through the redemption which is in Christ Jesus, whom God displayed publicly as a propitiation in His blood through faith. This was to demonstrate His righteousness, because in the forbearance of God He passed over the sins previously committed.

—Rom. 3:23–25

JUSTIFY

To render, show, or regard as just or innocent; to free, release, and make just as one who is not subject to condemnation

Justification is God's declaration that the one who receives Christ is made innocent and freed from his or her own inability to be right with God and the consequences of that separation or condition.

It is a gift by His grace. A person can't earn a gift. There's nothing we do to deserve His justification. We are justified 100 percent before the throne of God. It's hard to wrap our minds around the concept of being that clean because we're so acquainted with the law of sin and death. We can take Him at His word—He sees no fault in us.

Coming into Alignment with the Law Fulfilled

The great news of the gospel of Jesus Christ is that He fulfilled the Law that demanded works and behavior to fulfill it. God knew it would be impossible for fallen mankind to fulfill the Law, so He sent His Son to do it for us.

> [N]evertheless knowing that a man is not justified by works of the Law but through faith in Christ Jesus, even we have believed in Christ Jesus, so that we may be justified by faith in Christ and not by the works of the Law; since by the works of the Law no flesh will be justified.
>
> —Gal. 2:16

We can be satisfied—or made full or perfectly right with God—through our faith in Christ. As we receive Christ's life in place of ours, the scales we want to balance get balanced for us *permanently*. The scales of imbalance—measuring, not being enough on our own—have been removed from us. Those who are in Christ no longer have to prove their worth. It is secured through faith in God's Son, who already paid the price for our separation and our futility. We can live from the position of redemption that God gave us through daily faith in Christ.

We are no longer gauging our salvation on whether or not we've done this right or that wrong. We now live under the grace of Christ, who fulfilled the Law on our behalf. God came to set us free from sin. Our thoughts should be God-conscious, not sin-conscious. Romans 8:12–13 says, *"[W]e are under obligation, not to the flesh, to live according to the flesh—for if you are living according to the flesh, you must die; but if by the Spirit you are putting to death the deeds of the body, you will live."* You have been set free from focusing on your sin; it only produces more death. If you know Jesus Christ personally, you have been freed from death (thinking on sin) and can be consumed by the Spirit who produces life.

We already have what we need through Christ's payment on the cross and the resurrection. It's not that we can sin freely and it's all okay—it's that we have a Savior who paid for that sin, and now we can freely come to God without shame. We have the power to bring our sin to God, repent, and come back into full alignment with God's understanding of us. The quicker we do that, the quicker the life of the Spirit has full control. But the more we wrestle with measuring and weighing ourselves in the balance, the more we focus on getting over our sin areas and staying in sin instead of yielding to God. As John 3:6 says, *"That which is born of the flesh is flesh, and that which is born of the Spirit is spirit."*

In Rhiannon's situation, when she learned about the blame and shame principle, the Lord revealed to her that her "not enough" feelings were obviously condemnation and judgment under the Law. The Law measures, and no one can ever fulfill it. Coming to realize that the weightiness of what she was living under was a legitimate spiritual reality was incredibly validating for her. The Lord also showed her that her inescapable and painful feelings were actually the sting of shame. She tried to cope with her shame by bringing her feelings to her husband with the hopes of proving to herself that she wasn't the issue. (Do you see the blame at work here?) When shame interfered with Rhiannon's course work, she could only deny the pain and try to perform on top of it. Ultimately, she was running wildly from self-blame and shame to try to preserve herself as much as she could.

Even as Christians, we think, *Oh, I just need to get more in the Word. I need to know how to avoid this. I need more accountability with other people.* All these ideas are attempts to get into alignment using our own strength. Aligning myself with God is a matter of dying to self. It's about yielding—yielding control over our own souls. We must learn how to be like a grain of wheat that falls into the ground and dies—to lies, to our own self-lack and self-strength—and instead come into agreement with what God has already done and said (John 12:24–26).

. . . .

Aligning myself with God is a matter of dying to self.

. . . .

We are accustomed to coping. We do not realize that current behavior is rooted in past pain. Because God is redemptive, He wants to reveal the lies we believe, and He invites us to repent. What aligns us is agreement with God. If we believe something that isn't in agreement with God, we can't put agreement on top of disagreement. But that's what we try to do when we have lies we believe deep in our souls. We try to renew our minds to the truth, but there isn't room for it because we've already yielded to another belief, just like Adam and Eve.

We can't retain our beliefs and yield to the truth of what God is giving us. That's double-mindedness, and a double-minded person is unstable in all his or her ways (James 1:7–8). The only way to make room for the truth is to find the lie we've been believing and come out of agreement with it so we can come into full agreement with God, just like we talked about in Chapter 1. This is true repentance.

Equipped with this new understanding, it was easy for Rhiannon to get a breakthrough during her Exchange with the Lord. Jesus fulfilled every jot and tittle of the Law for her, and the Law was only a placeholder (or tutor) until she was ready to truly know Jesus in that place. She willingly exchanged the judgment of not being enough and cast out the lies for the truth that she is the child of faith and inheritance described in Galatians 4. The Lord defines Rhiannon by her faith in Jesus, not by anything that happened to her. All His promises are accessible to her, and she's received a new heart.

(That was the literal picture He gave her—replacing her heart with His.)

Listen to what she says about her experience:

> I don't measure my own worth anymore, and it actually helps me see problems with greater discernment. Living with measurement automatically meant I was the problem. That became frustrating. Now I have the head and heart space to traverse inside the landscape of conflict unrestrained. I legitimately don't feel the sting of abandonment anymore. That pain had been there for as long as I could remember, but the pain is totally gone.

Now when Rhiannon encounters a frustrating circumstance in her marriage, she can have hard conversations and have them quickly. She is grounded in a non-self-preoccupied reality and can think logically. She has room in her heart to acknowledge real feelings, move into true forgiveness, and release her experience to Jesus.

Rhiannon acknowledges that the transformation is a miracle. When she thinks about her future now, it feels bright. If she feels herself starting to get down, she remembers she's a child of promise and that God has already said yes to a good future for her. It's not dependent on her. Knowing this, she says, is super freeing. Jesus paid the price already. She can have intimacy in that place too. She can feel His presence and affirmation that she's on the right track, and He encourages her to keep going.

As you go through this process on your own—letting God reveal your "stuck places" and points of pain and then going to Him for revelation of the truth—don't be afraid to look at the places you may feel shame. It can be painful to look at shame, and because of that, we sometimes try to dress up our presence with the Lord and act holy. Because of blame and shame, we are afraid of what God might show us, and it feels better to hide. Shame tells you not to come into the presence of the Lord. Isn't that the grandest scheme of all, that the Enemy tells us we're shameful and prevents us from wanting to enter into the presence of a Holy God?

God's presence is the best place to go. He accepts you and loves you no matter what. The sacrificial blood of Jesus covers you. Pain is not bad. Pain is what causes you to go to the doctor to find out why you're sick. This same idea can be applied spiritually. When you have pain, something is out of order, and God has an answer. Go to the pain.

When Adam and Eve chose to eat from the Tree of the Knowledge of Good and Evil, they chose separation from God's loving provision instead of immediately repenting and restoring their relationship with Him.

Born into this fallen world, we fill ourselves with our own beliefs based on this world, but the world can only quell our loneliness temporarily. This independence is woven into our nature, and while we are still made in His image and likeness, we are consumed with measuring ourselves against others, balancing our scales, and keeping a ledger of our sins, all of which keep us separated from God.

The cross and resurrection restored our broken communion with God so we can now enjoy divine intimacy. There is great hope for redemption over every lost and broken thing. We can kick out the false belief systems, throw away coping mechanisms, and make room for God's fullness by living in absolute dependence on God. The Law, the measuring system, cannot restore us to our native state. Blame and shame cannot restore us to our native state. Only Jesus can restore us to our native state so our lives can radiate the beauty of the Lord and rule and reign on the earth the way God intended.

Personal Processing

Meditate on These Verses

For even though they knew God, they did not honor Him as God or give thanks, but they became futile in their speculations, and their foolish heart was darkened. Professing to be wise, they became fools, and exchanged the glory of the incorruptible God for an image in the form of corruptible man.

—Rom. 1:21–23

"For God knows that in the day you eat from it your eyes will be opened, and you will be like God, knowing good and evil." When the woman saw that the tree was good for food, and that it was a delight to the eyes, and that the tree was desirable to make one wise, she took from its fruit and ate; and she gave also to her husband with her, and he ate. Then the eyes of both of them were opened, and they knew that they were naked; and they sewed fig leaves together and made themselves loin coverings. He said, "I heard the sound of You in the garden, and I was afraid because I was naked; so I hid myself."

—Gen. 3:5–7, 10

1. What are you lacking that you really want to see God fill up?

2. Ask the Lord to show you what it would look like if His fullness dwelt in that place of lack. Write it down.

3. Ask God to reveal to you what it would be like to not have to strive to get your needs met. Take forty-five seconds, and let the Holy Spirit show you. Journal your thoughts.

4. Just today, how often did you react to something out of fear of being measured? How often did you measure others?

5. Think of a situation recently when you felt shame and reacted with blame. Have you been living your life independently from God? If you have, go to Him with your repentance, and surrender your life to all that God is. Acknowledge to the Lord that until now, all your choices have been fruitless and you desire to bring your mind, will, and emotions under His authority and love.

6. Sit quietly for two minutes, and ask God to show you where you're being robbed of knowing Him and his goodness. Journal what God reveals.

Prayer

Declare this out loud.

God, I really want to live a redemptive life. I am tired of defeat, tired of shame, tired of coping. I am tired of being weighed down by the heaviness of making life happen from my own strength. God, I really want to have wholeness and completeness in the power of God. I repent for choosing blame and coping mechanisms in the face of my own lack, and I accept that You made me with lack so I can be filled up in You. Come fill me up now. Thank You for Your sacrifice that took away my measuring scales. Renew my mind every day so I can live without measurement and grow in the knowledge of You in every circumstance. Amen.

Chapter 3

BODY, SOUL, SPIRIT LIVING FROM THE INSIDE OUT

For those who are according to the flesh set their minds on the things of the flesh, but those who are according to the Spirit, the things of the Spirit. For the mind set on the flesh is death, but the mind set on the Spirit is life and peace, because the mind set on the flesh is hostile toward God; for it does not subject itself to the law of God, for it is not even able to do so, and those who are in the flesh cannot please God.

—Rom 8:5–8

At this point in the book, you may have gone through a deep struggle. It is painful to hear about God's fullness and envision a life where that is possible and yet look at your life and wonder how. The absolute beauty of this process is that God is for you, and He is with you. This chapter is where the rubber meets the road.

God created us with a body, soul, and spirit. In 1 Thessalonians 5:23, Paul writes, *"Now may the God of peace Himself sanctify you entirely; and may your spirit and soul and body be preserved complete, without blame at the coming of our Lord Jesus Christ."* God is concerned that these three aspects of our humanity stay integrally connected and submitted in correct order. When we are born again, we receive the power of the gospel, Jesus Christ. His Spirit lives in us.

In the book *Journeying Towards the Spiritual*, Watchman Nee explained it like this:

> The soul makes it possible for the spirit and the body to communicate and to cooperate. The work of the soul is to keep these two in their proper order so that they may not lose their right relationship—namely, that the lowest, the body, may be subjected to the spirit, and that the highest, the spirit, may govern the body through the soul.[1]

Nee is essentially talking about living from the inside out (being led first from the spirit) as opposed to living from the outside in (being led first by your senses or your soul).

---

1. Watchman Nee, *Journeying Towards the Spiritual* (New York: Christian Fellowship Publishers, 2006), 4.

Body, Soul, and Spirit Diagram

Once people yield to Christ as Savior and Lord, the Holy Spirit dwells in their spirit, their innermost being. He is truth and will always lead us to the truth. He is our eternal connection to commune with God 24/7. Remember, because we are justified—made completely righteous— we are always able to come to God's throne and get what we need. We can learn how to respond to the Holy Spirit within us, accessing the life of God, the peace of God, and the grace of God. Life's circumstances and our fallen human nature no longer have to dictate how we respond. We can respond to the life of God within us from a place of fullness.

Until we die, we will have to contend with things that offend our bodies and our souls, but we can choose a higher way to respond, drawing from the Spirit who dwells within us. It takes discipline to stop living from our emotions, our own understanding, and our outward behavior and start living from our rightful position in Christ. Because Christ lives in us through the Holy Spirit, we have the ability to choose life and not death. Deuteronomy 30:15 says, *"See, I have set before you today life and prosperity, and death and adversity."* Again, it's a matter of choosing who we will glorify—God or Satan. There is no in-between.

The good news is that we have the perfect model for how to live from the inside out. Jesus lived in the world only doing what He saw His Father doing. He didn't react to what was happening around Him, and He didn't allow earthly surroundings to impact whether He yielded to His Father or not. The world didn't dictate Christ's decisions. Isaiah 11:3 prophesies of Jesus, *"He will not judge by what His eyes see, nor make a decision by what His ears hear."*

We are accustomed to living from our souls—allowing ourselves to be guided by our will, mind, and emotions—but when we do that, we are drawing from our *own* understanding and strength instead of from the life of God within us. The purpose of this chapter is to learn how these three aspects—body, soul, and spirit—interact and influence one another so we can discover how to respond in the ways of God, the only source of true life. That is how we will fulfill Genesis 1:28, to be fruitful and subdue the earth according to His life within us.

Body

The body is the physical, visible form of ourselves. Our bodies allow us to recognize the differences between us. It is an encasement. I once heard someone describe it as an "earth suit." I think that's a good description.

Before Christ, our physical senses and our own understanding dictated how we lived. We lived from the outside in. Situations come from the outside, first impacting our bodies. Living life according to our physical senses says that what we see, hear, feel, taste, and smell is the true substance of life. We have to learn to go beyond our senses through our souls to engage the truth of God in our spirits.

Reacting to physical stimuli is what animals do. That's living from the outside in. Most people make assumptions about situations based on what they see or feel. Have you ever experienced hearing something and thought immediately what that meant, but it didn't mean that at all? Or have you seen something that looked like something in particular, but it really wasn't that at all? Imagine a war veteran at a fireworks show. His senses hear the explosion sounds, smell the burning paper and gunpowder, and see flashes of bright lights. His senses are telling his brain that he's in a life-threatening situation, but in reality, he's safe. Our senses, as much as they help us navigate the natural realm, do not determine our reality.

Living from your body is survival of the fittest. If I've got to survive and something comes in that doesn't feel good, doesn't look good, and doesn't seem right, I'm going to protect myself and quickly decide what it means because of how it made me feel. Now I've decided to yield my will to that immediate, earthly, or worldly belief. That's how strongholds (deeply embedded belief systems) happen. That is how most people live their lives.

It causes us to perceive future situations through that protective belief, strengthening the stronghold and keeping us from being able to see, hear, and believe that what God says is true.

We don't want to live subjecting our soul and spirit to the physical reactions of our bodies. But as humans, we are constricted by our flesh. So how do we order our bodies to the Spirit within us? We submit our physical senses that are connected to our soul's interpretation of those senses to our spirit where the Holy Spirit dwells in us. That is called communing with God. We are choosing to let God into what we sense and have Him tell us what it is, what it means, and how to respond.

Soul

The second aspect of our being as humans is our soul. The soul is made up of our mind, will, and emotions. Combined, they give us our personalities. The body is the tangible part of us; the soul is the intangible part. It is in the soul where we process what we encounter, determine how it makes us feel, decide what we think, and then choose whether or not to act. The soul also houses the conscience where we store our experiences and decisions.

The conscience is the part of the soul that works as a moral compass to help us discern right or wrong, good or evil. It's an interface or connecter between the soul and the spirit. Your conscience isn't automatically aligned with the Holy Spirit, however. The conscience is a battlefield where the accuser comes in and tries to condemn you. The fallen conscience feels something is off and measures right and wrong in human understanding, trying to balance the scales by reacting with shame, blame, hiding, or striving. Our conscience needs to be cleansed because our natural bent is still to live under the Law, even after salvation (1 John 3:19–20).

A conscience can also be seared. Instead of letting the conviction of the Spirit shift and change a person, the conscience becomes scarred from disobedience and self-justification, unable to receive renewal. Conviction can no longer take hold (1 Tim. 4:2). But the Lord made our conscience to sense when something is off to cause us to realize our need for Him. Hebrews 9:14 shows us this difference. The blood of Christ, the life source of God in us, cleanses our conscience from dead works and makes us alive to God. The cleansed conscience goes straight to God to get our needs met to make things right and holy, which is life, instead of looking to self or others (dead works). Just like the other members of your being, you can submit your conscience to the Holy Spirit for renewal.

Belief systems are built on how we define our experiences and feelings. This belief system is held in our conscience, and as we move through life, it is triggered when we encounter new situations. In Chapter 1 we talked about belief systems getting built by your surroundings and your own reactions. Parents, the environment you were in, genetics, personality, authority figures (teachers, pastors), friends, culture, and the enemy all shaped our belief system as children. Some of them are influencing us even now.

Our soul is a filter for processing everything we encounter in our daily life. Most of us think our value and identity are found in the soul realm since that is where we think, emote, and choose to behave. Because we were separated from God after the Fall, we did life according to the mandates of the external world. The external world is ruled by the *"prince of the power of the air, of the spirit that is now working in the sons of disobedience. Among them we too all formerly lived in the lusts of our flesh"* (Eph. 2:2–3). At the foundation, our thought life has been primarily shaped by the nature of our enemy, Satan, who has influenced every aspect of the world with his need to be worshipped instead of God. The other influencing factors are then built on that foundation.

The mind that is set on this world is, by definition, hostile toward God (Rom. 8:5–8). Satan is hostile to God. Anything that is not in alignment with God is producing hostility or resistance. Sometimes we wonder why we're not hearing God or why we feel God is resisting us. Often it's because there's something we're entertaining that's hostile to God. God's not going to entertain that with us.

A major place of hostility in Christians is their unbelief toward receiving the fullness of what Christ did for them on the cross. When we act out of our human souls, we pull from our own humanity—our self-strength—with no life or power from God. That is why we react to an offense with anger or self-righteousness. We do not have to live from our souls any longer. In Christ, we have the opportunity to go into our spirits and receive power to respond like Him. We get to live from a new identity in Christ instead of from self-effort and measurement.

The difference between living from the outside in and living from the inside out is clear. The fruits of living these two lifestyles are opposite. I want to tell you about a young man named Keane who grew up worried about being perfect. He struggled with the identity he knew he should have access to by faith, but instead, all he could feel were his imperfections and inadequacies. When issues arose, Keane wanted to interact well with his family and reconcile with them, but often he found himself ignoring his problems until they got worse. By responding to life out of his soul, he kept doing what he didn't want to do. Paul talks about this in Romans 7:21 (NIV): *"So I find this law at work: Although I want to do good, evil is right there with me."*

When Keane got an Exchange, God showed him that he was wrestling with fear of making mistakes. God showed him a memory of growing up with family members who shamed and punished him for making mistakes in his schoolwork. He was so afraid of making mistakes that it affected his relationships with family members and how he viewed himself as a man. He believed the lie that because he made mistakes, he was a mistake. Keane was measuring himself from the outside in—judging himself by his outer life and allowing mistakes and inadequacies to define him. Those judgments had a lot of power because he agreed with them. He was trying to have perfect control of his soul through sheer, human willpower. He was trying to reach a level of perfection that was reserved for Jesus Christ alone.

Hebrews 5:13–14 says, *"For everyone who partakes only of milk is not accustomed to the word of righteousness, for he is an infant. But solid food is for the mature, who because of practice have their senses trained to discern good and evil."* It takes practice to discern when we're depending on our own understanding and when we're asking the Lord what He says about situations. We get to *"be quick to hear [God], slow to speak and slow to anger [act, decide]; for the anger [act, decision] of man does not achieve the righteousness of God"* (James 1:19–20).

Sometimes, like Keane, we get so in tune with our souls that we measure our spirituality by how our soul is functioning instead of by what God secured through His Son—our complete justification—no matter how we behave. Deciding to believe in the security of our new nature in Christ instead of how our souls are functioning is a choice.

. . . .

Deciding to believe in the security of our new nature in Christ instead of how our souls are functioning is a choice.

. . . .

Statistically, we know that when we're in a small group of people, there's usually someone in the group who's addicted to pornography. The world tells us it's okay to want to satisfy our need this way. Because that idea is pervasive, it seems right. Then we start walking with the Lord, and other believers say, "Hey, that's actually not good for you. Don't look at porn. It's lust; it's objectifying women." That's a new way of thinking, so we have to go to the Word of God and find out what He says. We then have to come out of agreement with the world, repent for that sin, and begin to yield to what God says. This takes renewing our minds in a consistent and disciplined way so we can walk in discernment.

What I see happening in many young people is that they come to Christ, they're serving the Lord, and then they experience a place of stress or conflict. They feel the temptation to soothe themselves, so they think, "Hey, you know what? I'm tired. I've had a long day, and this is comforting to me. I want to go back to this old thing." We think that's who we are because of our feelings, so we start to step back into that habit. We don't realize that's not who we are anymore.

When we're born again and alive to God, we're no longer slaves to sin. Our old selves were forgiven, and our sin nature was removed. We're now a new creation, no longer driven by our behavior and our old sin nature. That temptation and pressure isn't who we are in our spirit; it's residue of the old. We still have a tendency to own it, though. We think, *Oh no! I just looked at porn, and now I must feel shame about myself.* Then the cycle continues. Our behavior will usually get worse the more we go into a shame cycle about it and let it determine our identity.

Nothing about your behavior *determines* your identity. Think of it this way. If you spend time in a house where someone smokes, the clothes you were wearing will smell like cigarettes when you get home. It wasn't you; it was residual from your being there. The cross of Christ is resurrection power and gives us the power to be out from under those ashes, that smell, and that familiarity with sin. It has no power over you because in the core of your being, you are truly righteous in Christ.

When we tolerate sin cycles, it leads to increased shame, more rebellion, and destruction, and it can even end up in adultery. What could happen in that moment of looking at porn is to take our shame to the Lord, repent, and return to God's love for us. We then can submit to our brothers and sisters like it says in James 5:16. We can say, "Hey, I was stressed out and decided to look at some porn. Will you help me? Will you pray for me? That's not who I am. I'm struggling with an old pattern." If I realize Christ has already paid the price for my sin nature, that I'm clean in the deepest, truest part of my identity in my spirit, that I'm justified because of Christ's payment in my place, that I'm alive to God 24/7, then my sin doesn't limit me from being able to access Him. This positions me to receive His truth in that area of my life.

The Word of God is critical in retraining our thought life to the truth of who God is, who we are in Him, and how to divide our soul and spirit in our identity. On a daily basis I have to realign myself to my eternal design in order to respond from that nature and not what is familiar to me or what the world tells me. That comes from being in the Word and agreeing with it.

Our will is the power to choose. When we live every day led by the Spirit and renew our minds and subdue our emotions to the truth, we are strengthening our will to make choices that align with God. We are no longer limited to our own understanding and ability to deal with life. We have the ability to connect with God. That is so powerful—to live life beyond our limitations by moving from what we feel, think, and have previously experienced into our spirit, with the Word of God to train the members of our body to live unto righteousness (Rom. 6:12–13).

Spirit

The third aspect of our being is our spirit. Our spirit is the truest part of who we are, the core of how God made us.

We have a human spirit that we're born with where the likeness of God's eternal nature was formed. But apart from Christ, or before He comes into our lives, our spirit is dead to God. Ephesians 2:5 tells us we were dead in our transgressions. We may have been made for eternity, but our connection to God was dead. We were no longer able to be alive in Him. When we were alienated from God, we were hostile to life in Him (Col. 1:21–22). We were acting out of self-life, separated from Him.

When we give our life to God through Christ, the Holy Spirit comes to live in our spirit. We awaken to the things of God and are able to commune with Him. It's still a choice, but now we actually have the ability to have that relationship.

When God imputed (put) Christ into our spirit, He declared us justified because the only Righteous One, Jesus Christ, paid the price for our unrighteousness. He alone could stand in the gap for each one to make a way to be made right and declared just through faith in Christ.

Through justification God credited us with the complete righteousness of Christ's Spirit. Righteousness means being made right with God, which happened through faith in Christ. Does that mean we're only righteous when we are able to connect with our spirit? Do we lose our right standing with or acceptance from God when we're not obeying? No. Why? Because He said of His children, *"and I give eternal life to them, and they will never perish; and no one will snatch them out of My hand"* (John 10:28). Christ's justification of us is permanent. God's choice to clothe us in Christ's righteousness through our salvation is permanent. When we are faithless, He remains faithful.

RIGHTEOUS

Having the character or quality of being right or just according to God's own character and nature.

For in it the righteousness of God is revealed from faith to faith; as it is written, "BUT THE RIGHTEOUS MAN SHALL LIVE BY FAITH."

—Rom. 1:17

But now apart from the Law the righteousness of God has been manifested, being witnessed by the Law and the Prophets, even the righteousness of God through faith in Jesus Christ for all those who believe; for there is no distinction.

—Rom. 3:21–22

Our righteousness is not based on our ability to always know what's right or do what's right. In fact, it's not based on our abilities at all. It's based on the One who is righteous and gave His righteousness to us. You have to come to grips with the reality that you have no capacity in yourself to bring God-life or be righteous. It was given to you by the imputing of Christ's nature through salvation. God does not measure us by worldly standards. When God looks at us, He sees His Son.

Our position has permanently changed. We are now spiritually alive forever, even when we don't access it. We are hidden with Christ in God (Col. 3:3). Where Christ is, we are. Christ is seated in heavenly places, and so are we (Eph. 2:6). Our position is no longer on earth trying to connect to heaven. We are in Christ, in God, seated with them.

Take forty-five seconds, and ask the Lord to show you what that looks and feels like. You might want to write your answers in a journal so you can go back to them. I do these forty-five-second times with God a lot, asking Him to reveal (receive supernatural understanding) the truths I read in the Bible. That might be new for you, but in Christ, you can see and hear by the Spirit. Once you access a revelation like that, it becomes yours, and you can continue accessing it in your daily life—you just have to ask.

Being seated in the heavens has nothing to do with our ability to maintain our righteousness. It only has to do with the righteousness of God now living in our spirit.

· · · · · · · · · · · · · · · · · ·

Being seated in the heavens has nothing to do with our ability to maintain our righteousness.

· · · · · · · · · · · · · · · · ·

The next logical question is this: If we teach people these truths, can't they just sin all the more? You might even be feeling this prick you, afraid that if you really accept this truth, you will have no pressure to obey God. It's an interesting question, but Paul covers the answer in Romans 6:1: *"What shall we say then? Are we to continue in sin so that grace may increase?"*

If we truly understand what God has done for us, we will not want to sin. As we renew our minds about who God is, about His deep abiding love for us, and about the fullness of life we can have by yielding to Him, we will be compelled to show love to Him through our obedience. The love of Christ constrains us so we don't live for ourselves but for Him who died and rose again on our behalf (2 Cor. 5:15). The more time we spend with Him, fellowshipping with His love for us, the more we begin to throw off sin and self-life and become conformed to His ways.

As we are maturing in our faith in these truths, we will sin less. This is the transforming process called sanctification. It doesn't happen all at once, but as we give ourselves to God's Word, yielding to His nature and ways, we will become more and more like Him.

With the Spirit inside of us, we are alive to God again. We don't have to act or react from our old nature. Just because we feel something doesn't mean it's true. In fact, we are to subdue—take control of—our thoughts, our reactions, our words to the Spirit in us by God's Word to see how God sees them, not based on our darkened and limited understanding. We can fellowship with Him all day, every day with no limits. We are filled with God's Spirit and live from the inside out. We learn to respond from our spirit and not our flesh. We respond to the Holy Spirit by gaining revelation and then acting on faith.

So how do we live from the inside (the imputed righteousness of our spirit) out instead of the outside (the pressures of the world affecting our members) in? How do we produce righteousness in our body and soul from the connection to our spirit?

Revelation and Faith

"*For in it* [the gospel], *the righteousness of God is revealed from faith to faith*" (Rom. 1:17). In the gospel—through Christ, through the good news—the righteousness of God is revealed. Apart from faith in Christ, we cannot achieve the righteousness of God. Your initial moment of salvation happened through true revelation in your spirit—we have to be in God's Word to see the truth so faith in God and His ways can be ignited. Without revelation, we can't have faith. As we posture ourselves more and more in the gospel, we grow in knowing Him. Then revelation of Him comes alive in us, and our faith increases.

"But to this day whenever Moses is read, a veil lies over their heart; but whenever a person turns to the Lord, the veil is taken away" (2 Cor. 3:15–16). So not only when you are born again is that scripture true, but each time you turn to the Lord, the veil is taken away. In the initial coming into unity with Christ, the veil has already been torn and split so we can have full access to heaven. However, when we choose to operate from our old way (self-life), our hearts become veiled again to God, and we can only produce dead works.

When we yield to the Spirit in us through faith, we can live from God's understanding and heart and bring life into our situations. That is how we access the spiritual blessings of heaven. Faith is an action. It means I am choosing to act on what I see revealed in God's Word. A true believer can only know God by faith, by choosing to believe in and act upon what God says in His Word.

We can't embrace the revealed will of God and His righteousness when we listen to our soul, the Enemy, the world, or the voices of influence in our lives. I encourage you to stop kicking against what God did for you through Christ on the cross and receive it. Our former selves still want to contribute something of value to righteousness and redemption, but scripture is clear: there is nothing good in us apart from God (Rom. 7:18).

. . . .

Our former selves still want to contribute something of value to righteousness and redemption, but scripture is clear: there is nothing good in us apart from God.

. . . .

I share with people that understanding Romans 7:18 was the second-best revelation I ever received from God because it took all the striving and pressure I felt to be a "good Christian" and removed it. I was so relieved! I'd been failing miserably anyway. I could get out from under that judgment of trying to become like Christ and now learn how to live as one with Christ.

Faith comes by revelation. Faith does not come by our ability to reason—our ability to even understand—apart from God. There's no amount of mental exercise we can do, no amount of good works, and no amount of those kinds of acts that are going to save us. Faith comes from revelation, and revelation comes by hearing . . . and hearing . . . and hearing . . . and hearing the Word of God. There is no shortcut. Faith is not going to come another way.

Now faith brings our hopes into reality and becomes the foundation needed to acquire the things we long for. It is all the evidence required to prove what is still unseen. And without faith living within us it would be impossible to please God. For we come to God in faith knowing that he is real and that he rewards the faith of those who passionately seek him.

—Heb. 11:1, 6 (TPT)

Faith causes you to put your hope in God and then act upon that hope as if it already is true because it is true in heaven. Faith is the key to connecting our heart and will to God's. Everything in our walk is dependent on this so we can make transactions from our souls to His life in us. Faith is the act of our will to believe God is able and will do what He says. Faith repositions us from having to make something happen to believing God has already made provision for everything He says in His Word. This is easy to believe when you have revelation. When I believe what He has said to me, I can stand on faith.

As I position myself to absorb the Word and allow it to become "light" to me, I gain revelation. I grow in faith as I spend time in the Word wrestling out His will until my will yields to His. Once I know what God is saying, then by faith I can do my part through obeying Him and waiting for Him to fulfill His Word.

· · · · · · · · · · · · · · · ·

I grow in faith as I spend time in the Word wrestling out His will until my will yields to His.

· · · · · · · · · · · · · · · ·

There is a huge price to pay to have faith like this. It takes time to renew your mind to agree with God's Word. Romans 10:17 says, *"So faith comes from hearing, and hearing by the word of Christ."* There are several meanings for *word* in Greek; one is *rhema*, or "with revelation." Remember, Hebrews 5:13–14 says that because of practicing the Word of righteousness, our senses are trained to discern good and evil. We have to hear it and hear it, practice it and practice it.

God rewards those who diligently seek Him. Every time we choose to wrestle out an area of unbelief, we build our faith. It's the same as working out. The more we do it, the stronger we become. The more we wrestle out our faith with the Lord, the stronger our faith in Him becomes.

Because of our choice to have faith in God, we must know what He says is true and then stand on that truth no matter what it looks like or costs. We have been shaped by our nature before Christ and by this world's systems since birth. We are more familiar with those ways until the Lord's ways come to life for us.

When I was preparing to spend a year in China, I had to raise about $20,000. I had never done anything like that before. I had to grow my faith to be able to truly believe God would do that. I spent hours listening to teachings on faith, which was building my faith. Then one night I took Philippians 4:19, and for two hours I paced in my apartment speaking out that one verse until the lightbulb moment (revelation) came. I really believed that my God would supply all my needs according to His riches in glory in Christ Jesus. Two or three weeks after that, all $20,000 came in.

When we live an Exchanged life, we learn who we are in Christ and exchange the old way for the new, practicing repentance—changing our mind and heart when lies are revealed to us. We make these exchanges continuously throughout our life in order to come into the fullness of who we are meant to be in Christ.

Every place we have lack, unfulfillment, and darkness, we believe in the old way in some place of our mind and heart. We need to turn from the lie of Satan, our enemy, and the world that is conformed to Satan's ways, and discover the truth of God's Word and His ways. Find a scripture (or two or three) and begin to declare the truth of it over your life until you have an aha moment—the lightbulb coming on. That is how faith increases.

Isaiah 55:9 says, *"For as the heavens are higher than the earth, so are My ways higher than your ways and My thoughts than your thoughts."* God's ways bring life and peace; Satan's ways bring destruction. We know God's ways are higher because of the quality of life they produce in us and on the earth. Satan has duped us into thinking the highest level of life is found in this world. Remember, he is a liar, and all he can do is lie (John 8:44). Do not believe him, but fight hard to find the truth so you can enter into a higher life.

John 8:31–32 (NLT) states, *"You are truly my disciples if you remain faithful to my teachings. And you will know the truth, and the truth will set you free."* You will be free from the torment of this world, bondages, and the lack we have been talking about—bad relationships, depression, sickness, no provision, fear, insecurities, and destruction. The more we learn to access the truth of heaven, the more we enter into the life we are meant to have.

Living in freedom is a life-long process. Learning to walk in Christ's provision is a daily adventure. Overcoming the old life is not easy, but once you experience the goodness of God in an area where you were in bondage, you realize He made you for so much more than this world can give. I exhort you to take up the challenge of being in God's Word regularly, yielding your own ways to His, and discover the peace and joy that transcends this world.

Abraham's Faith

In Romans 4:16–22, Paul writes about Abraham, our father in faith from the Old Testament. Abraham is a great example of someone who knew God, trusted God, and lived by faith—not his own understanding, feelings, or past experiences (although he did have moments when he didn't know how to walk out his faith). His story is the ultimate example of learning to live from the inside out. *"For this reason it is by faith, in order that it may be in accordance with grace, so that the promise will be guaranteed to all the descendants, not only to those who are of the Law, but also to those who are of the faith of Abraham, who is the father of us all"* (Rom. 4:16).

Paul says that even Abraham, a Hebrew, wasn't justified by his works. Abraham was righteous because he believed God. If righteousness came by works, then the relationship with God would be based on mankind's self-righteousness rather than righteousness that can only come from God. In God, we are all equal—no righteousness of our own, but instead needing Christ, the Righteous One, to be righteousness in us. This position requires every human to be reconciled by faith to God and yield to His nature and ways to truly live a life of worshipping Him. Our righteousness doesn't come because we help the little old lady cross the street or because we memorize ten Bible verses. It comes because we have put our trust in God.

Abraham believed God would keep His promise. Our faith gets proven and produces righteousness when we believe God is who He says He is and that He will do what He says He will do. We produce righteousness every time our soul wants to elevate ourselves but instead yields to God and says, "No, my hope is in God." Faith in and of itself is what God counts as righteousness. When we put our faith in God, that righteousness changes the atmosphere. Faith changes us and the atmosphere around us. Our obedience to believe God changes the atmosphere. Romans 4:17 says, *"(as it is written, 'A FATHER OF MANY NATIONS HAVE I MADE YOU') in the presence of Him whom he believed, even God, who gives life to the dead and calls into being that which does not exist."*

. . . .

Faith changes us and the atmosphere around us.

. . . .

Let's look at how Abraham lived out his faith. God made a promise to Abraham that he and his wife Sarah would have a child. They'd been infertile and now were old. How did Sarah respond? She laughed because she couldn't comprehend how that could happen when she considered the deadness of her womb (Rom. 4:19). She allowed the external, the physical, to dictate her belief in the truth of God's Word, His promise for their lives.

This is a great example because it shows us the challenge of contemplating the natural world in light of the promises of God. But Abraham believed God, *"who gives life to the dead and calls into being that which does not exist"* (Rom. 4:17).

In hope against hope he believed, so that he might become a father of many nations according to that which had been spoken, "SO SHALL YOUR DESCENDANTS BE." Without becoming weak in faith he contemplated his own body, now as good as dead since he was about a hundred years old, and the deadness of Sarah's womb.

—Rom. 4:18–19

77

Look at the faith Abraham exhibits here. He had to trust what he knew about God. He trusted that when God makes us a promise, it's based on who He is and His ability to do what He says despite the way things appear. Abraham wasn't in denial about their ability to have a son at their age. We read that he contemplated it. Instead of getting stuck on what he couldn't see or understand, he knew God was the Promisor and was able to perform what He said. Abraham could offer God his aged body and his wife's body and believe that since He promised it, He was able to do it. *"[Y]et, with respect to the promise of God, he did not waver in unbelief but grew strong in faith, giving glory to God, and being fully assured that what God had promised, He was able also to perform. THEREFORE IT WAS ALSO CREDITED TO HIM AS RIGHTEOUSNESS"* (Rom. 4:20–22).

Abraham had a revelation from God, the One who could overcome the natural order. If we only allow our faith to be in what we can see, we limit the realm of the impossibility that God wants to empower in us with faith. God is not limited to the way we think life works. He is supernatural, living beyond the boundaries of the natural. All things are possible for God as we access Him by faith. In our own limited understanding, we can't make sense of it, but we can take Him at His word.

We also see evidence of growth in Abraham's faith. It is a great example of the alignment we've been talking about throughout this book. We align with God's truth. Instead of being convinced that his physical body wouldn't be up for the task, Abraham remained strong in his faith in God's Word. In Genesis, we read more details of Abraham's story and how he didn't do it all correctly. He made some mistakes because sometimes he reverted back to his own understanding, but his faith and righteousness weren't based on his ability to not mess up. When he messed up, God didn't shame him; He convicted him, just as He convicts us of the truth that leads us to repentance. Repentance means to change our mind and realign with God. Abraham chose alignment, and it was reckoned to him as righteousness. The Lord gives us the same opportunity.

When we realize that God is more concerned with having a relationship with us than He is anything else, we can cease striving and allow Him to father us. We are His sons and daughters. How God dealt with Abraham is a great example of His parenting style. He isn't interested in punishing our mistakes. He's interested in wooing us to Himself, receiving us even in our sin so He can love us and lead us back into yieldedness to His nature and ways as His children. That is how we daily experience the deep love of God that brings fullness in our lives.

Changing the Way We Respond

How do we keep our thoughts from straying away from faith in God? First, in that moment, we must receive by faith our position in Christ that God has given us, which is His full redemption. Then we align ourselves, like we discussed in Chapter 2. The choices we make, the things we tell ourselves, create a pathway in our brains that can lead to life or death.

I can share one of the ways I go about aligning myself. When I realize my emotions aren't aligning with God, I stop and begin to talk to Him about what's going on. I spend a lot of time discipling people. Sometimes something a person says about their situation begins to bother me, but I don't know why. I might feel agitated or defensive and want to shut them down with a response that's abrupt. Because I've known the Lord a long time, it's easy for me to recognize this, but I still have to choose to yield to the Spirit of God in me. I begin dialoguing with the Lord in my spirit even while I'm still listening to the person. I tell the Lord I'm frustrated, and then I listen for His heart. I begin to hear His heart for the person, or because I know His nature is about love, I begin to shift my thoughts. Now I'm aligning with God. Now He can begin to bring wisdom and insight I wouldn't have had on my own. I'm aligning my thoughts with my position in Him.

The key is to get back in alignment with the righteousness of God that was secured for us by His goodness, and His goodness alone. That's why He's so worthy. If He's holding out somewhere on us and expecting us still to prove something, that's not any better than what we can do by ourselves.

Where did God leave things with Keane? God spoke to Keane and said, "I called you to be like Jesus, not to *be* Jesus." Keane exchanged the lies he believed for God's truth, and God gave him His reassurance that He didn't want perfection; He wanted Keane to have faith. The process the Lord was leading Keane into was about relationship, not about being right. This young man grew up thinking independence and doing the right thing were what qualified his right standing before God. The Lord cracked open Keane's heart and revealed to him that he actually has access to his justified nature all the time and can rest in that reality.

God wanted Keane's heart apart from what he could do for God. After Keane's Exchange, the Lord revealed His deep desire for moment-by-moment connection with him. This moment-by-moment connection is through the Holy Spirit in Keane (abiding in Keane's spirit and Keane choosing to stay in touch with that understanding). Faith began to express itself through Keane in the moment-by-moment yielding to the heart and voice of God instead of the presumption and independence of his own performance for God.

This Exchange began the breakthrough for Keane to understand Sonship through the finished work of Jesus. It became a process for Keane to retrain his heart through the power of Christ to slow down from the work and find contentment in the identity of being beloved of God. As the revelation of Sonship expressed itself in faith through this man, the layers of shame tied to his validation in works slowly were stripped away. He said yes to the process, not just to the single moment of revelation in his Exchange.

For Keane, weakness and uncertainty became catalysts to knowing God instead of striving in his humanity. As he began walking out these truths, he testified about reaching out to some family members and working out reconciliation. No longer was fear dictating his life; freedom was—freedom to be imperfect and weak but have the Perfect One, Christ, on the inside. This process of accepting his weakness, choosing first to set his mind and identity in Christ and then respond to life from there, is what it means to live from the inside out.

We are accustomed to making decisions in response to impulses of our soul and body. We used to only process life from the outside in. Living that way produces a resistance to the Lord because we're pulling from our human soul, not from the Holy Spirit.

God has redeemed us and put Christ in us so He can demonstrate to the world how amazing He is. When we yield to His authority in our lives and believe in His righteousness and grace to empower us, we will reveal Him to the world. When we decide to obey Christ in big and small ways, we are declaring Him to the worldly powers and principalities (Eph. 3). That gives us a bigger picture about our lives.

When we align with Him, it doesn't matter what we're called to be about in this life—ministry, parenting, truck driving, teaching school. It's about believing God. A homeless person can have more effect over powers and principalities than I can if that person believes God and responds in faith more than I do. Bringing order to the world has nothing to do with the positions God allows people to be in.

What brings true order is a believer believing God. So stand in the righteousness of God, imputed to you by grace, because of the justification through Christ in your life!

. . . .

What brings true order is a believer believing God.

. . . .

Personal Processing

Meditate on These Verses

And you were dead in your trespasses and sins, in which you formerly walked according to the course of this world, according to the prince of the power of the air, of the spirit that is now working in the sons of disobedience. Among them we too all formerly lived in the lusts of our flesh, indulging the desires of the flesh and of the mind, and were by nature children of wrath, even as the rest. But God, being rich in mercy, because of His great love with which He loved us, even when we were dead in our transgressions, made us alive together with Christ (by grace you have been saved), and raised us up with Him, and seated us with Him in the heavenly places in Christ Jesus, so that in the ages to come He might show the surpassing riches of His grace in kindness toward us in Christ Jesus.

—Eph. 2:1–7

And although you were formerly alienated and hostile in mind, engaged in evil deeds, yet He has now reconciled you in His fleshly body through death, in order to present you before Him holy and blameless and beyond reproach.

—Col. 1:21–22

For those who are according to the flesh set their minds on the things of the flesh, but those who are according to the Spirit, the things of the Spirit. For the mind set on the flesh is death, but the mind set on the Spirit is life and peace, because the mind set on the flesh is hostile toward God; for it does not subject itself to the law of God, for it is not even able to do so, and those who are in the flesh cannot please God.

—Rom. 8:5–8

For this reason it is by faith, in order that it may be in accordance with grace, so that the promise will be guaranteed to all the descendants, not only to those who are of the Law, but also to those who are of the faith of Abraham, who is the father of us all, (as it is written, "A FATHER OF MANY NATIONS HAVE I MADE YOU") in the presence of Him whom he believed, even God, who gives life to the dead and calls into being that which does not exist. In hope against hope he believed, so that he might become a father of many nations according to that which had been spoken, "SO SHALL YOUR DESCENDANTS BE." Without becoming weak in faith he contemplated his own body, now as good as dead since he was about a hundred years old, and the deadness of Sarah's womb; yet, with respect to the promise of God, he did not waver in unbelief but grew strong in faith, giving glory to God, and being fully assured that what God had promised, He was able also to perform. Therefore IT WAS ALSO CREDITED TO HIM AS RIGHTEOUSNESS.

—Rom. 4:16–22

1. Practice being in the presence of God. Think about the position that was purchased for you through the shed blood of Christ. Practice receiving that position out of His righteousness and goodness. This can be a powerful experience. Journal about your experience.

2. Is there a situation in your life where you need to align yourself with what God says versus what you're saying to yourself?

3. Know that through the Holy Spirit in you, you have power to agree with and obey God in that place and bring His glory. Continue to exercise the

first step above (receiving God's righteousness for you and your new position) in that situation and begin training your members to live out of what the Holy Spirit is showing you.

Prayer

Declare this out loud.

Lord Jesus, thank You for the gift of your Holy Spirit that resides in my spirit. I repent for where I have chosen to live out of my soul and have squelched Your Spirit in me. I choose right now to receive Your life-giving power through my spirit, and I submit my members to be trained by You. Teach me how to live out of the Spirit so I can know You and bring Your glory to the earth. Amen.

Chapter 4

LIFE IN THE HEAVENLIES

Therefore if you have been raised with Christ, keep seeking the things above, where Christ is, seated at the right hand of God. Set your mind on the things above, not on the things that are on earth. For you have died and your life is hidden with Christ in God.

—Col. 3:1–3

In the last chapter, we talked about the three parts of our being: body, soul, and spirit. We are well acquainted with our body and our soul (mind, will, and emotions). In this book, we are learning about the truest part of our identity: our spirit. This is a major shift for any human being because we are so in touch with what is physical and natural. Learning how to live primarily from a deeper place in our identity takes time and practice. We have to be trained by going into our spirit to discover how the truth of our identity, position, and purpose really comes to life. We are used to living unto ourselves, others, or the world. The Lord made mankind to expand His glory into another realm—earth. We are to reflect Him in and through our life. We have to come into agreement with Him about who we are, what we are to be about, and how to live that way, which is totally opposite of how we learned to live before we became believers.

> But God, being rich in mercy, because of His great love with which He loved us, even when we were dead in our transgressions, made us alive together with Christ (by grace you have been saved), and raised us up with Him, and seated us with Him in the heavenly places in Christ Jesus, so that in the ages to come He might show the surpassing riches of His grace in kindness toward us in Christ Jesus (emphasis added).
>
> —Eph. 2:4–7

Because of our justification in Christ, we are repositioned in Christ. He is seated in heaven with the Father, and now, because Christ is in us and we are in Him, we are seated there too. Our primary new position is in the throne room in heaven with Christ. We have 24/7 access to the atmosphere of heaven and the mercy and grace of God (Heb. 4:14–16). We are one with Christ, and we have been made right with God. This is our permanent position with Him.

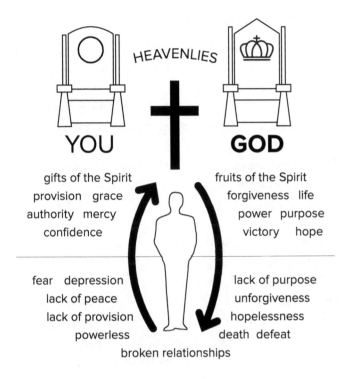

Heavenlies Diagram

As you read, hold this image in your mind. Although you are physically on the earth, you have access to all the treasures of heaven through Christ. You can "go up" in your spirit and get what you need from your Father in heaven. You get to know Him as Provider, Friend, Father, or however He wants to reveal Himself in your need. Then you can move through the natural, earthly realm with God's riches, power, and ways. This is a key way to live the Exchanged life.

What Is Heaven Like?

The heavenly places are mentioned twice in the book of Ephesians, first in Ephesians 1:3, *"Blessed be the God and Father of our Lord Jesus Christ, who has blessed us with every spiritual blessing in the heavenly places in Christ,"* and again in Ephesians 2:6, *"and raised us up with Him, and seated us with Him in the heavenly places in Christ Jesus."*

We've been talking about our need to renew our minds to the truth of the Word of God. We should always be thinking, *What does God say about this?* It is a great place to start searching the Word about heaven and who God is. We search the Word for spiritual understanding. When we read, we look for verses that reveal the nature of God, Christ, and the Holy Spirit. They are truth and the Creators of heaven. Who they are is what heaven is like. Then in the places we haven't believed what these verses tell us, we get to change our mind, or repent, and by faith choose to agree with God. We can begin to meditate on the truth, training our souls to believe what God says.

Think about the following questions, and make a list for each question's response: (1) What is heaven like? (2) What is God like? (3) How is that different from earth? (4) Which one would I rather be a citizen of?

Now that you've compared earth with heaven, take it one step deeper, and ask God to show you what heaven is like. Take forty-five seconds, and let the Lord show you in your spirit the answers to these questions:

- God, what does heaven look like and feel like?
- What would I experience right now if I were in heaven?

You are probably experiencing immeasurable joy, peace, worth, confidence, adventure, and provision. Remember, because you are seated in the heavenlies right now, you have access to all these things. I encourage you to come out of agreement with anything you have believed that puts a limit on your access to God's riches and come into agreement with the new truth you just received. Say, "God, I repent for believing _____ (the lie), and I come into agreement with what You just showed me: _____." Every time you agree with God, it strengthens your faith. Remember, it takes *faith* to walk with God.

Another example would be to ask the Lord what it looks like to not live under stress. This is an amazing question that allows people to encounter God's truth. Heaven has no stress. If we don't have experience with the truth of God, how can we walk in it, much less give it away to others?

We need to have these transactional encounters with God regularly, renewing our mind from being ruled by our outer selves (body and soul) to learning to live from our inner selves (spirit) in agreement with what God originally designed mankind to experience daily—an overcoming, supernatural life. When we lean on our own understanding, all we have to give to others is our own understanding. That produces measuring others, religious boxes to walk in, and self-strength with little power. It keeps us from communing with God, which is where transformational life is imparted to us.

We have to ask the Lord to show us so we can experience it. Then we can be a pipeline to release it on earth. When we apprehend truth by faith, our new reality becomes our new way of life. I can access no stress because I'm actually seated in the peace of Christ in heaven more than the reality of me being here. Heaven is my true home now. Since there's no stress there, I can access that because I'm in Christ, and Christ is in me.

When you imagine your seat in heaven, see yourself seated face-to-face with the Lord in the same way the Bible says Moses was (Exod. 33:11). The veil has been taken away. We can have a conversation and relationship with Him just as we would a friend. This is the biblical reality of seeing ourselves in relationship with God rather than thinking we're somewhere out of sight or away from the Lord. The beauty of this is that the more we live this way, the more we know God and are living in His fullness. We'll get to the point that it's all going to be about Him because that's what heaven is. We will be communing with Him 100 percent of the time.

Engaging these truths and revelations about heaven causes us to realize that we already have access to heaven now. I have access now to not being afraid, insecure, or self-conscious. Let me give you an example of this. Because I'm secure in Christ, I'm not looking to others to make me feel secure. When I receive criticism, when something at work doesn't happen the way I planned it, or when I've made a messy mistake, I don't respond by trying to hide. I don't feel compelled to defend myself to others. I don't feel ashamed of my lack or the fact that I just made a mistake in front of all my coworkers. We would probably be shocked at how much time people spend doing similar mental gymnastics. The revelation of heaven is that none of us will be self-conscious—the same way Adam and Eve weren't self-conscious before the Fall. In Christ, we have gained a new position, a new identity, and a new authority.

Position in Christ

We now have a new position in Christ. What is that position? Being seated in heavenly places in Christ. Don't forget that last part—"in Christ." When we're thinking about how we are responding to a situation or person, we can remember, *I'm responding to the Lord, and I'm in Christ.* That's a pretty good combination for victory! I'm already in Christ, have His full provision, and I'm responding as unto God who loves me and gave Himself up for me through His Son. This is our new position all the time. In this new position, there is no distance between me and God because He is outside of time and space. Heaven is outside of time and space.

In this new position in Christ before God, He has restored us completely. So when we're not feeling okay, what do we need to do? We need to go before God. We may be here in this world, but we need to see ourselves standing before God.

Therefore, since we have a great high priest who has passed through the heavens, Jesus the Son of God, let us hold fast our confession. For we do not have a high priest who cannot sympathize with our weaknesses, but One who has been tempted in all things as we are, yet without sin. Therefore let us draw near with confidence to the throne of grace, so that we may receive mercy and find grace to help in time of need.

—Heb. 4:14–16

This is where Exchanges take place, at the throne of grace. This is so important. This is the Exchange that has to be the foundation of everything. We have to shift from limiting ourselves to this world and get in our rightful position before God. When we come before Him, what do we have? We have His peace, His righteousness, and His perspective—not ours. We can stop trying to find our own identity and provision and just take His. Being in Christ before the Lord makes all things possible.

. . . .

We have to shift from limiting ourselves to this world and get in our rightful position before God.

. . . .

That's what John 15:4 is all about. *"Abide in Me, and I in you. As the branch cannot bear fruit of itself unless it abides in the vine, so neither can you unless you abide in Me."* Abiding—that's what it means to stand in position. Abide. Remain. Continue. Establish. I'm going to establish in my mind, will, and emotions by faith that my position is in Him. I'm getting that firmed up before I try to figure out how I'm going to pay my bills, before I try to figure out how I'm going to pray for you, and before I try to figure out how I'm going to take care of my family. I need to get in position so I have miracle-working power to raise kids and miracle-working power to pay my bills and impact the world.

Don't we all want to live beyond paying our bills? God gave us His miracle-working power to live a miraculous life. Let's do it!

Identity in Christ

Living with access to the heavenlies also gives us a new identity. We are now sons and daughters of the King of the universe. We are made in His image, righteous through Christ. This is a radical transformation of who we are. We've been totally changed. Our new identity is like no one else's. We become brand new in the Lord. Galatians 2:20 says, *"I have been crucified with Christ; and it is no longer I who live, but Christ lives in me; and the life which I now live in the flesh I live by faith in the Son of God, who loved me and gave Himself up for me."*

We are now spiritually seated before the throne 24/7. Paul tells us we're seated in the heavenly places in Christ. Our nature is changed. That new nature gives us a new citizenship. This new citizenship means we have new rules to live by, but those rules are the rights of heaven. They aren't bound by earthly limitations. The law on earth is limited to what man can do. Because the Enemy has the right to work in the sons of disobedience (Eph. 2:2), there can be a spirit of death and heaviness on our lives that robs and steals from us.

But we have new rules that take us up into the heavenlies where we have everything we need for life and godliness. We have provision, peace, joy, and love. We have all the rights of Jesus Christ to everything that's in heaven. That now becomes my right to experience here and now. It's my right to have provision. I want to be clear, though. It's only my right because of Jesus. I can have an expectation of those needs being met because I'm born again and I dwell in heavenly places, in Christ Jesus.

It is from this new home that we have a new family, a

new source of authority, and a new way of seeing ourselves even on earth. I am now fully a child of God even more than I am a child of my earthly family. God sees me the same as His Son. I am a son or daughter grafted into the same inheritance.

Joint Heirs

We are no longer slaves to the Law, but through our faith, we are joint heirs with Christ (Rom. 8:17). An heir is someone who is legally entitled to someone else's property after that person dies. Because Christ died in our place, those who receive His death and resurrection now become joint heirs as God's children. We get the same inheritance as Christ.

What is Christ's inheritance? Ultimately, His inheritance is to glorify His Father. So our inheritance is to glorify God in all things. We have the power and authority to glorify God above all else. We were created to radiate the beauty of God. Everything is about God. Think about how God the Father sees, feels, and interacts with Jesus the Son. As a child of God, you are now a co-heir with Christ. Every way the Father relates to the Son is how He relates to you.

. . . .

Every way the Father relates to the Son is how He relates to you.

. . . .

You have 24/7 access to God's throne, His place of presence. The same way He longs to talk to His Son, He longs to talk to you and bless you. The same way Christ humbled

Himself before His Father, always yielding His will to obey, is the same posture we are to have with God since we are co-heirs with Christ. When we take this posture, we can have access to all of heaven's provision, power, and authority. This is the highest and most precious right or privilege we could ever be given.

Romans 8 and Ephesians 1 are two great chapters to help you understand the empowerment of God to His children. When we yield our life to God, we become conduits of heaven, releasing the fullness of God-life all around us. The primary way we glorify God is to honor and obey Him in likeness to His Son. Jesus glorified the Father above all else, in every way.

Our salvation gives us the privilege of being able to demonstrate and magnify all that God is in our everyday life. It's a privilege to now be freed from bondage—freed from a life constrained by my own resources, to be able to come into God's throne room 24/7 and receive kindness for my humanity, love for my brokenness, and empowerment for my weakness. If we don't receive this amazing gift, we will not find the fullness of God's design for us.

We're supposed to be so full of the nature and identity of God that everywhere we go, it brings that essence on the earth. This causes the atmosphere on earth to shift, causing heaven to invade the lives of those around us. We want all mankind to know God, which is why we should care about being joint heirs. It's not so we can have blessings because that would be an end unto ourselves. I care about being a joint heir so I can fulfill God's original plan for me, which is to express His nature. It's not about me. Our fulfillment is in seeing God worshipped and glorified.

. . . .

I care about being a joint heir so I can fulfill God's original plan for me, which is to express His nature.

. . . .

When each of us radiates God's beauty, we express His light and glory in ways unique to us, like a diamond or a snowflake. God is intentionally pursuing individuals because He longs for their specific expression of Him to be on display. We see different aspects of God through each one of us. For instance, God has gifted me with a way of helping people discover their purpose or strengths. I can sit and listen to someone talk about their life, and because of God's design in my life, I can see by the Spirit order, vision, and direction for that person. On the other hand, I don't have a strong gift of organization or ruling. Recently, our ministry needed that gifting because we had grown, and I didn't know how to build structure for it. The Lord brought several people to us in new ways, and I recognized that gift in them. It's been amazing to watch them provide what I could not. That is how Habakkuk 2:14 will be accomplished. *"For the earth will be filled with the knowledge of the glory of the LORD, as the waters cover the sea."* It will be through us.

As joint heirs rightly fit together, the fullness of God is brilliantly revealed. For example, in Romans 12:4–9, Paul lists seven designs God has given to individuals. We call them redemptive gifts. We believe each person has been given one or two of these gifts as the primary way they are gifted to relate to life. I have a friend who has a teaching gift. Teachers love to spend hours researching the Word in order to share the revelation that causes others to know the beauty of the richness of God's nature and ways. I love to teach the Word, but my primary gifts are giver and exhorter. An exhorter loves to be out with people sharing the Word and helping people see the application of the Word to their daily lives. I rarely sit as long as my friend does to revel in the joy of study. Both of these are important to the kingdom but have different rhythms and expressions. God loves both.

Not Slaves, but Sons and Daughters

Romans 8:14–16 says, *"For all who are being led by the Spirit of God, these are sons of God. For you have not received a spirit of slavery leading to fear again, but you have received a spirit of adoption as sons by which we cry out, 'Abba! Father!' The Spirit Himself testifies with our spirit that we are children of God."* On earth, what you receive is slavery. Before you come to Christ, you are born into sin. Sin is an offense to God, which brings guilt as its consequence. Without Christ in our life, we are in bondage to sin and its slavery. There is no other way. Without Christ, it is impossible to please God. The consequence of sin is death, separation from God.

The earth is enslaved under the rule of Satan (Eph. 2:2). That is why to be born of God—to be saved—is so unbelievably gracious of God. Apart from God, not only are we ruled personally by a sin (self) nature, but we live on a planet that is ruled by God's enemy, Satan. Remember, God gave the earth to mankind, before sin, to rule over, but we chose to respond to Satan instead. How kind, generous, and brilliant of God to already have a plan to restore us through His Son! Those who yield to God, receive Christ, and are filled with His Spirit are freed from slavery and can now live as sons and daughters of God. Geneva learned this lesson during her Exchange experience. I want to tell you her story.

When she was seven years old, Geneva believed the lie that she was a good liar after her father, in a moment of anger, told her she was a better liar than her sister. "I didn't know I was a good liar, so that was a shock to me," she told me. What had been childhood experimentation with lying became a pattern for her. She explains it this way:

> I used lying to escape consequences, to embellish stories, to impress people, and to get what I felt like I needed without doing the work required for it. In high school, I essentially lived a double life—one for my parents and church and the other for my friends at school. I had a lot of shame about the lying but seemed powerless to stop completely. Whenever I was backed into a corner, I lied with boldness to escape consequences. I used anger to bully people who didn't believe me.

Geneva was living out the lie she believed about herself. Her identity was rooted in the lie, and she was a slave to her sin. Remember that Romans 8 tells us we don't have an identity of slavery any longer. That's not our identity anymore. I am a son, I am a daughter, and therefore I can cry "Abba! Father!"

We get to have intimacy with God all the time. Anything that comes into our lives that brings oppression or makes us feel enslaved should be a red flag, a place of spiritual confrontation. By confrontation I mean taking it to the Lord and asking Him, "What is this? Where did it come from, and what do I do about it?" We must confront anything that wants to enslave us. Do not tolerate it because you have been set free. I'm not necessarily talking about feeling enslaved by other people, although it can manifest through another person. It's spiritual. It's a belief system that tells us we deserve to remain a slave to the values of the world, to our emotions, and to our resources.

The spirit of adoption is when we cry "Abba! Father!" to God. We are no longer subject to the values of the world; we are now empowered by the Holy Spirit in us to step into the position God has given us through His Son. We refuse to be enslaved again, and we refuse to be left only to our man-made ability to try to be free and full. Relying on our man-made abilities doesn't get us very far, as Geneva soon realized.

In her thirties, Geneva was dealing with a lot of anger and sought out an Exchange ministry session. The Lord took her back to this encounter with her father. She said, "I told Jesus that my father said I was a good liar and asked Him for the truth. He said, 'Oh sweetie, you're not a good liar, you're a truth-teller. Your daddy just doesn't know you as well as I do.' I received that truth and forgave my father easily as the Lord showed me how scared and helpless he had felt."

Geneva asked the Lord to show her a redemptive picture of her identity. "I saw myself and Jesus walking along a road and coming upon a man who looked dead. I knelt down and pulled from my backpack a honey-type substance, which I fed to the man with a golden spoon. The man revived and praised the Lord."

Geneva said this Exchange changed her life. "I knew in my heart that the truth God had given me about my identity was right. I embraced it and began to speak it about myself. I repented and forgave myself for all the lying and the messes

I had made." Geneva said that after all this, she pressed more into her call as a Bible teacher and discipler with greater passion as she now had confidence in her identity as a truth-teller. "I know I wouldn't be doing what I'm doing in ministry today if it hadn't been for that Exchange."

Geneva eventually embraced her role as a co-heir and daughter of the Most High. If at first you struggle with feeling like you're not a part of God's family, then make sure you've yielded your life to Christ. Then ask the Lord why you are doubting. Let the Lord reveal the lies you may believe so you can repent of them and renew your mind to what God says. If there is any place in your experiences or concepts that doesn't line up with what is true in the Word, then search the Word to get God's truth, repent, and come out of agreement with what your earthly realm experience has been. Then you are able to come into agreement with what God says. There can be a lot of warfare against your feeling accepted by God and people, so you must get this foundational truth settled with God in order to grow into fullness.

Understanding this is an important part of being a joint heir. It is your right in Christ, not because you earned it. If we don't feel like we're part of God's family, we can't receive our inheritance. In order to receive our inheritance, we have to agree with the spirit of adoption because God said it is true. His Word trumps anything we experience or feel. We can ask the Lord to show us in the spirit what it is like to be part of the family of God. We can say, "God, You adopted me; it says that in the Word. Now I want to see and feel that in the heavenly places." And when He gives us that, we're more able to believe it. *I am part of His family. I do deserve this. I do get the full inheritance that Christ gets.*

We want to receive this because it changes the way we

see life, and we are able to respond in power. I can feel peace knowing that all God intended me to be, in my design and my destiny, is one who radiates the glory and the beauty of who He is.

. . . .

I can feel peace knowing that all God intended me to be, in my design and my destiny, is one who radiates the glory and the beauty of who He is.

. . . .

When we get depressed or feel alone and lost, we can remind ourselves that we are citizens of heaven. We are sons and daughters of the King of kings. Even though we may have had difficulty in our earthly families, we can now discover and believe in God's redemption of what family should be. That's why we need to be renewed; we may not know how or even want to claim our adoption into God's family because of our family of origin.

To be able to receive our adoption, we must address what happened in our earthly families that is causing resistance in us to believe in our heavenly position. We must recognize that our earthly experience is not our heavenly opportunity. Then we need to ask the Lord to show us where our "stuck place" began, what we believed because of it, and what His truth is to replace what we believed. Once we repent for believing the earthly lie and agree with God's truth, we can receive the fullness of sonship in that area. There might be many areas of unbelief blocking our faith related to being sons or daughters of God. We can deal with each one as it is revealed.

It's essential that we confront the lie we believed that robbed and stole from us, which we know ultimately was the Enemy. Where did the lie begin, and how did it manifest itself in our day-to-day life as we were growing up? What is causing a resistance in us that's keeping us from believing that Father God is waiting in heaven for us to come and say, for example, "I really need to know you as a gentle Father because my dad wasn't gentle." Then God can come to you and say, "All right. This is what it looks like."

We've talked about the process of making an Exchange, and I'll continue sharing the process over the chapters of this book. This is another situation where an Exchange is part of living in the fullness of Christ. We take our current memories and beliefs of a painful situation to the Lord, and He replaces them. For example, let's say your father was an alcoholic and at times he would rage. As a result, you may have a lot of fear that is carried over into your view of God. Maybe you don't have confidence that you really have access to God when you didn't even have access to your dad because he was unavailable or you were afraid of him.

In an Exchange, the facilitator might say, "Lord, would You show this person where You were in the midst of that?" He might show you that you spent time with an aunt who was super loving, receiving of you, gentle, kind, and other qualities you needed. That was an expression of God. It might not have been your father, but God did put someone in your life who expressed His nature to you. You can ask the Lord, "God, what does gentleness look like from You? How do I engage that?" He may say, "Well, I actually gave you an aunt growing up who was gentle and kind. She was my expression of love and gentleness to you."

Your father may not have had those experiences in his

own life that would enable him to be like that for you. Now you can have mercy toward your dad, forgive him, and separate your dad's behavior from who God is and wants to be to you. Once you deal with the earthly experiences that have tainted your trust in God, you will be able to take your place in God's family. Then you can experience the fullness of being blessed *"with every spiritual blessing in the heavenly places"* (Eph. 1:3).

If we don't confront the "stuck place," we don't get to replace the experience we had on earth with the reality of God's heart in heaven. When we do confront it and see God's provision and truth instead, we can be freed from the lie that is robbing us of faith in God.

Authority in Christ

Living with access to the heavenlies also gives us a new authority in Christ. Mark 16:15-18 tells us we have resurrection power—the power to heal the sick, to love, to turn darkness into light, to preach the gospel, to bless instead of curse, to shift atmospheres by displaying God's nature.

Jesus had authority because of the truths in the following two passages:

Have this attitude in yourselves which was also in Christ Jesus, who, although He existed in the form of God, did not regard equality with God a thing to be grasped, but emptied Himself, taking the form of a bond-servant, and being made in the likeness of men. Being found in appearance as a man, He humbled Himself by becoming obedient to the point of death, even death on a cross. For this reason also, God highly exalted Him, and bestowed on Him the name which is above every name, so that at the name of Jesus EVERY KNEE WILL BOW, of those who are in heaven and on earth and under the earth, and that every tongue will confess that Jesus Christ is Lord, to the glory of God the Father.

—Phil. 2:5–11

But whatever things were gain to me, those things I have counted as loss for the sake of Christ. More than that, I count all things to be loss in view of the surpassing value of knowing Christ Jesus my Lord, for whom I have suffered the loss of all things, and count them but rubbish so that I may gain Christ, and may be found in Him, not having a righteousness of my own derived from the Law, but that which is through faith in Christ, the righteousness which comes from God on the basis of faith, that I may know Him and the power of His resurrection and the fellowship of His sufferings, being conformed to His death; in order that I may attain to the resurrection from the dead.

—Phil. 3:7-11

Paul had a powerful transformational encounter with God on the road to Damascus that totally reset his understanding of God. These two passages are Paul's response to that encounter. He understood that knowing God reordered who really had authority, and that power and authority would only come in his life in true holiness by yielding his life to God.

Paul had seen the disciples perform miracles, but now he knew where that authority came from. John 5:30 says, *"I can do nothing on My own initiative. As I hear, I judge; and My judgment is just, because I do not seek My own will, but the will of Him who sent Me."* Jesus yielded His life to the Father even though He was the Son of God. He demonstrated to us how to live a life of authority and power through John 5:30. Even He laid down His right to live in His own strength and instead lived in submission to His Father, receiving power and authority from Him. The justification of Jesus has secured our admission to the heavenly realm. We are no longer primarily citizens of earth. We're citizens of heaven. This is our truest nature.

Being a citizen of a certain nation has requirements. We must either have been born there or have chosen by law to give up our rights to other nations in order to come under the rule of the nation we want to live in. When we live in a place, we must know the laws of that country in order to obey them as a citizen is legally bound to yield to the laws of the land.

We have laws in the earthly realm and in the heavenly realm. Because we were born on earth, we're familiar with and live under these earthly laws. With our new citizenship, we must lay down the rules of earth as our primary way of living. We have to learn the new laws—the new ways and rules of engagement.

When we learn the new rules, we find life. We live in newness. We are new creatures living a new life. That is how it feels when you've been born again. When you are living according to heavenly laws, you experience freedom, the fruit of the Spirit, and the power of the Spirit. When you live according to earth, you feel constricted, sometimes so much that you feel like you're in prison.

I'm an American, so obviously I'm used to American laws. But when I went to China, the laws and customs weren't the same. In fact, some were totally opposite. I had to learn enough of the laws of that land at the level of my living there so I could abide by the laws and not do something illegal.

Some of my American friends went into deep depression there because they couldn't understand Chinese ways. They didn't like them because their Westernization pressed against it, and they wouldn't let go of their American mind-set while on Chinese soil. They struggled and struggled and struggled. For example, it was a normal practice for many Chinese people to call foreigners white devils. Before we went to China, our trainers told us this and what the phrase was in Chinese. Many of my fellow workers were offended when they heard this phrase used toward them. They let it wear them down and ended up depressed.

I had decided before I went there that although I was an American, I would live respectfully of the Chinese when I was in China. None of it bothered me. I didn't have to understand what they did or said. I didn't have to agree with it. I just needed to yield to my identity in God and trust Him. I believe that's why I never struggled with depression while I was there. I actually thrived because it caused me to depend on the Lord much more. Above any earthly land, I chose to be submitted to God's land—His ways—and I was able to love the Chinese people, not be offended, and actually see several Chinese give their lives to Christ.

We have to learn what the ways of heaven are and what our rights are. We have new rights as citizens of heaven. We have a right to ask God without Him finding fault with us. We have the right to have peace.

What are some of these rights as a believer? We are now sons and daughters of Creator God, Father God, who is merciful, kind, good, just, true, giving, full of peace, all-powerful, forgiving, and so much more. We have a right to all He is and to everything in heaven. Our right is no longer about getting our way but about having access to how good God is and to His immeasurable love that He wants to pour out on all creation.

Second Corinthians 5:18–20 describes God's heart toward mankind and His will that all things be reconciled to Him. We now have the right (privilege) to be His ambassadors. We get to represent Him in this world, both to mankind and the Enemy, that God is the only true God, the only one able to fulfill us. We are authorized to represent the Lord to speak on His behalf in alignment with His nature and ways.

Because of this shift in citizenship, our power source is not limited to our own strength. Let me say that again. Our source of power isn't limited to our own strength anymore. We now have a supernatural power source. We have a new citizenship, a new identity, and a new power source.

It's time for us to see ourselves from another perspective— to see ourselves as God sees us. We are seeing ourselves in Christ. We live with God's pleasure over our lives. We no longer live under punishment. If He finished it on the cross, then I'd like to be finished with it too. I don't want to keep punishing myself, and I don't want to punish you either. This is where we live now; this is our new nature.

Under the new law, our power source has changed. On earth, we had to depend on ourselves, but with faith, we connect to the new power source, which is in heaven and in my spirit. His name is Jesus Christ. That's why I keep using the term *make exchanges* because we're used to making decisions ourselves. We have to keep coming to the Lord and making an exchange of what we think we know about living life for what He knows about living life.

It's harder sometimes in America than when I was in China because I didn't know how to get around in China. There, I was especially dependent on God. But here, I think I know how to do it. I think I know the rules and can get around. I can make it from day to day, but how many of us would admit that sometimes we're not making it very well. We get stuck. That's okay. We're in process and will be making exchanges for the rest of our lives, continually choosing to know and depend on God. We want to know His way because His way is always life.

We have to choose today which one we're going to serve—life or death. There is no in-between. As a culture, we've been confused about that. We must have thought there was some gray area, but we need to get really honest and clear. We're choosing either life or death—God or the Enemy and self. I want to choose life, building a history and a reservoir of life so I am always ready to be God's ambassador on earth.

The authority I have in Christ isn't just for me but for my life to impact others so they can be reconciled to God too. When I choose not to align with the redemption God has brought into my life, I don't have the power to exercise my God-given authority to impact others so they can be alive and free too. That's selfish of me. To not live in the fullness of the salvation God has given us is not loving. God's love and salvation cannot be kept to ourselves. That's not true redemption. The authority we have in Christ should always be bringing transformation to us because we are His ambassadors.

He's allowing these "stuck places" to continue in our lives so we press into Him and get to know more of Him. We get to experience a fresh download of His love, not only for us but for others. That's really what He wants. He wants to show His immeasurable love for us, and He wants us to share it with others.

Living It Out

Trials are the platform for knowing God. Everything in our life is for one thing—to know Him. If you don't get anything else out of this book, I hope you get that. Use the circumstances of your life as opportunities to know God; it will change everything.

. . . .

Use the circumstances of your life as opportunities to know God.

. . . .

About seventy-five times in the book of Ezekiel, the Lord says, "I did this" or "that happened" so *they would know Me.* To know Him means we experience what He experienced. He suffered, so we will too. It's how we access the Lord and His reality in our suffering that brings a maturity we can't attain any other way.

To know Jesus is to understand what He knew—what He learned, what He engaged His Father in through suffering, through trials, through death, but also through the joy of fellowshipping and eating with Him. All aspects of a relationship are what cause you to really know someone.

Trials and tribulations are the opportunity for us to depend on Him because we cannot overcome them apart from Him. We want to get to a place where we stop being threatened by problems. God does not expect us to have a perfectly smooth life. He wants friendship with us, and He wants to get the old way of living through independence off us so we can experience friendship with Him.

Through the process we learn patience, waiting on God (Rom. 5:3–5). The Word tells us to be of good courage and wait on the Lord. It develops Christ's character in us as we learn to wait on Him. He exposes things in order to woo us to Him for relationship, to know His amazing love. He's not exposing them to shame us. It's because He loves us and has something else for us, and He really, really wants to give it to us. We don't have to convince Him. We don't have to talk Him into it, but we do have to be willing to wait on Him to reveal it out of His love because He isn't a machine. It's about relationship.

That is why we can exult, why we can leap about ecstatically when confronted with a problem because it's a chance for us to get to know God, and God gets to show Himself to the world. Isn't that what we want to do, to show Him to the world, His glory filling the earth? Demonstrate God in all areas of your life. When we have a problem, our lives are the platform for demonstrating Him through our character and our responses and through Him showing up and doing something we can't do ourselves. Through the process of dying, we tap into His resources, and we know and demonstrate Him.

Living in the heavenlies means we are living in two realms at once. That sounds abstract, but this concept has a great impact on how you live every day. Living from the heavenlies means becoming a responder to God. When we face a situation on earth that isn't what heaven is like (losing a job, for example) we come to our seat in the heavens and present our need to God. Instead of reacting only to our circumstances, taking charge, and trying to fix the situation, we can come back to the truths in this chapter and meditate on who we are in Him. We are sons and daughters. We are ambassadors. We are co-heirs with Christ.

. . . .

Living from the heavenlies means becoming a responder to God.

. . . .

Spend time in the Word looking up scriptures that train you in the truth of what you hear from God about your need, and then respond to what He shows you by coming out of agreement with self and aligning with His truth. Then, by faith, you will receive His power in you to live in obedience to what He says and who He is.

If you are struggling to have faith after working through this process, ask the Lord if you have any hidden judgments about Him. Sometimes we cannot apprehend faith in God because we believe a lie about Him. If you continue the Exchange process, He will be faithful to reveal it to you.

When we gain possession of our new identity, our new position, and our new authority, we learn how to access the life of heaven. We learn to rely not on our own strength to make life happen the way we think it should. Our growing reliance on God increases by spending time before His throne where we have been given total access.

Personal Processing

Meditate on These Verses

Blessed be the God and Father of our Lord Jesus Christ, who has blessed us with every spiritual blessing in the heavenly places in Christ.

—Eph. 1:3

[E]ven when we were dead in our transgressions, made us alive together with Christ (by grace you have been saved), and raised us up with Him, and seated us with Him in the heavenly places in Christ Jesus, so that in the ages to come He might show the surpassing riches of His grace in kindness toward us in Christ Jesus.

—Eph. 2:5–7

For our citizenship is in heaven, from which also we eagerly wait for a Savior, the Lord Jesus Christ; who will transform the body of our humble state into conformity with the body of His glory, by the exertion of the power that He has even to subject all things to Himself.

—Phil. 3:20–21

The Spirit Himself testifies with our spirit that we are children of God, and if children, heirs also, heirs of God and fellow heirs with Christ, if indeed we suffer with Him so that we may also be glorified with Him.

—Rom. 8:16–17

1. Imagine yourself sitting in heaven in front of God. How do you see yourself there? Let yourself explore the vastness of heaven.

2. Write down at least twenty blessings of heaven that you have a right to. (If you don't know what you have a right to, how are you going to access it?) Reread Ephesians 1:3–14.

3. Contrast that list with what the earth realm is like. Which realm do you want to be walking in?

4. Over the next week, ask the Lord to show you what it means that you have a new position, identity, and authority through Him. Write down what He shows you, and begin to engage that place in faith by declaring it over yourself.

Prayer

Declare this out loud.

God, I repent for limiting You on earth because I've not experienced You in heaven. God, I choose to stretch myself. I long to know You more in heavenly places. I choose to receive Your fullness and ask You to become as real to me on earth as You are in heaven. I want to pour You out on earth and bring earth back to Your original intent. Amen.

Chapter 5

STRONGHOLDS

For though we walk in the flesh, we do not war according to the flesh, for the weapons of our warfare are not of the flesh, but divinely powerful for the destruction of fortresses. We are destroying speculations and every lofty thing raised up against the knowledge of God, and we are taking every thought captive to the obedience of Christ, and we are ready to punish all disobedience, whenever your obedience is complete.

—2 Cor. 10:3–6

Are you encouraged that as a believer, you now sit in the heavenlies with your Father, Christ, and the Holy Spirit? How powerful is that new position, identity, and authority we now have in Christ! The same position, identity of sonship, and authority that Christ has are what you have as a believer. We have all the rights of Jesus Christ to everything that's in heaven. There are things that can hinder our ability to believe that these blessings and abilities are ours and thus limit our ability to walk in them. These are called strongholds.

Identifying the strongholds in our lives and using supernatural weapons to tear them down are critical for us to walk in fullness. We partner with the Lord to bring down strongholds that are keeping out His glory and beauty, the life source we so desperately need and were made for.

Strongholds are developed when we rely on our own strength to balance our scales. Our scales get out of balance when something happens to us that reveals our areas of lack. We then tend to use our human skills to justify our insufficiencies. Being insufficient isn't the problem; it's the behaviors we adopt to cope with them. Remember, God made us to need Him. We were created with lack so we would be dependent on Him.

. . . .

**Being insufficient isn't the problem;
it's the behaviors we adopt to cope
with them.**

. . . .

My mom taught me to be hyper-responsible. After I had been in ministry for about seven years, I had a nine-month season where the Lord was stripping me of my independence and self-strength. Romans 3:12 (NLT) really got ahold of me. It says, *"All have turned away; all have become useless. No one does good, not a single one."* I had to sit with the Lord for a while on that truth until revelation—the lightbulb—came on. Once I realized that God loved me apart from anything I could bring to the table, I was set free.

Remember, this was the second-best revelation I ever got

next to needing Jesus to be my Savior and Lord; God was well aware that there was no good thing in me, nothing that could produce good (God's good). It set me free from striving. What a gift! God released me from something I couldn't do anyway *and* gave the gift of goodness to me by putting Christ in me.

Now, because Christ is in me, I can look at my "stuck places" from a position of faith that I am already securely God's child and that He has what I need to pull down beliefs and situations that have tainted my faith in Him and the fullness He wants me to walk in.

What Is a Stronghold?

Many translations of the Bible use the word *fortress* or *fortification* instead of *stronghold* (Isa. 17:3–4; Hosea 10:13–15). Let's define the word *stronghold* in layman's terms. Webster has this definition of *stronghold*:

1. a fortified place: a place of security or survival

2. a place dominated by a particular group or marked by a particular characteristic[2]

I would like to suggest a *spiritual* definition of the word *stronghold*:

1. well-trodden neutral pathways that facilitate habitual actions and behaviors

2. the result of decisions made throughout a life course . . .

---

2. "stronghold," *Merriam-Webster*, https://www.merriam-webster.com/dictionary/stronghold.

- that were made in human strength as a response to a perceived lack
- so that now those choices have become a default operating system
- that is so entrenched it has taken on a supernatural quality

Every time we choose to believe something that does not align with what God says is true, it is like putting a brick in the wall of our strongholds. Every time we reason a situation in our own minds, every time we react from our own emotions, every time we choose with our will to do it our own way (living out of our soul), we are building the wall of independence around our hearts instead of having a relationship with God. We build the wall, consequently blocking ourselves behind it so we cannot receive from God what He has to give us for our situation. We are not able to experience His love and provision in our daily life.

One of the key ways we can see strongholds at work is through coping mechanisms or coping patterns. These are ways we have learned to make up for our lack or protect ourselves in situations that reveal our lack or insufficiencies. In our mind, this makes us feel safe, secure, or in control. When we feel vulnerable and don't know how to access the truth in God, we are driven to find some way to cope that hides the pain or fear of experiencing the shame of lack.

The more we reinforce that coping pattern, the stronger it becomes in our belief systems. It empowers the stronghold, strengthening the hold of the Enemy in that area of our lives. It becomes a supernaturally empowered place of belief. The only way to deal with those places in our lives is with the supernatural weapons of God. To defeat the supernatural work of the Enemy, we must use the supernatural power of God.

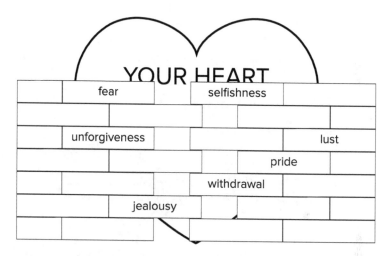

Stronghold Diagram

Some examples of strongholds are pride, lust, fear, independence, withdrawal, and jealousy. These strongholds become so familiar that we don't even realize they are present. We aren't able to see that anything in our thinking or behavior is wrong or disordered because the responses have become a part of the fabric of our existence. As a matter of fact, they seem so right that we will fight to the death with people who believe differently. While we aren't always able to see the stronghold, it is a major force in influencing how we think and what we do. Even though we don't always realize we are stuck, we probably feel some kind of pain that is not fulfilling.

Strongholds do two things: they keep things in, and they keep things out. What do strongholds keep out? The knowledge of God. I'm not referring to intellectual knowledge or what doctrine tells us. I'm talking about experiential knowledge—having experiences with God and living in communion with Him. Whatever natural tools or skills we rely on—tools based on our ability to cope with life—we need to declare that they are not useful anymore. Not only are they not useful, they are actually hurting us because they separate us from God and keep us in bondage, unable to live the life of fullness God has for every human being.

. . . .

Strongholds do two things: they keep things in, and they keep things out.

. . . .

We may lean on our intelligence or our craftiness and our ability to scheme and find the loophole. We may lean on our emotions, which were developed through protective reactions or even modeled for us by our parents or others. Again, it goes back to the whole idea of balances. We try to figure out a way to balance the scales of discomfort in our situations so we can win, self-protect, and come out okay.

It's important that we identify the stronghold so we can know what revelation of God is needed to overcome that place of unbelief. That happens in an Exchange when we ask the Lord what the stronghold is that's blocking us. Then He shows us the redemptive truth of how He sees us or the situation. We must get the correlation of the revelation of who God is in the area of a worldly weapon that we've been using so we can make an exchange.

I want to tell you about Mark because the evidence and effects of a stronghold in his life were especially evident. Mark is a reserved and adaptable person who appeared to easily adjust to difficulties. On the outside, no one would say that was a damaging way to live. However, on the inside, Mark's adaptability was actually the evidence of a poverty mind-set stronghold, a deeply rooted belief that he would never have enough or be enough, and so he must work to the bone in order to scrape by.

Mark grew up to be a hard and diligent man, never wanting to stir the waters. He saw that his mother never complained about lack in anything but just put her head down and kept moving. He learned, *if a person does you wrong, get over it and keep moving. If your job mistreats you, get over it and keep moving. If you lose something that was precious to you, get over it and keep moving.* These values may not strike you as wrong. In fact, they are looked highly upon in our world today, but later you'll read how they reaped death in Mark's life.

Proverbs 14:12 says, *"There is a way which seems right to a man, but its end is the way of death."* This is a description of strongholds—our beliefs, thoughts, and values seem right, but they aren't in alignment with God so they lead us to death, or separation from God. Remember, life is from God, to God, and in God; everything else is death.

How Strongholds Are Built

Stages of Life

From the earliest age, we begin building strongholds. Even in the womb, we are being impacted by our parents' emotions and words. As we continue to move through the early years of life, we form our views and responses to everyday experiences. We build strongholds through our own reasoning and self-protection in daily situations in order to build a safe belief system that we think will protect and prosper us.

These behaviors take on different expressions as we grow into adulthood. We figure out how to use all kinds of tools to help us cope with life with the goal of being okay or making it.

0–2 Years Old

We are born into selfishness under the Law because of Adam and Eve's choice to sin. All our actions as infants are about getting our needs met. Feed me. Change me. Hold me. Me, me, me. Our entire universe is focused on ourselves and our needs (food, diaper change, being held). Strongholds are being formed, even at this young age, built through self-strength.

2–4 Years Old

We continue to strengthen self as the center. We aren't inclined to share. Mine, mine, mine. Feelings of shame can begin to form. The word *no* is used frequently. Strongholds at this age are built through self-management.

4–12 Years Old

Enter jealousy, fear, anger, impatience, rejection. Strongholds for this age group are built through self-justification.

12+ Years Old

Lust, rebellion, withdrawal, bitterness, rage, and greed are the ways self-gratification is used to build strongholds. A person in this age group has an intricate collage of thoughts and behaviors that are increasingly related, which then builds on strongholds already laid.

Adding More Bricks

Let's look at 2 Corinthians 10:3–6 again.

> *For though we walk in the flesh, we do not war according to the flesh, for the weapons of our warfare are not of the flesh, but divinely powerful for the destruction of fortresses. We are destroying speculations and every lofty thing raised up against the knowledge of God, and we are taking every thought captive to the obedience of Christ, and we are ready to punish all disobedience, whenever your obedience is complete.*

Two specific things—*lofty thoughts* and *speculations*—are instrumental in creating and building up strongholds. The New International Version of the Bible uses the words *arguments* and *pretensions*. I previously used the words *reasoning* and *self-protection*. These are the weapons the world uses against the knowledge of God. They are the building blocks of strongholds or fortresses. Here's how.

Arguments—or speculations—come from human reasoning. Pretensions—lofty thoughts—come from pride. For example, think of how we manage our budgets. I know everyone doesn't act this way, but many people do. We think we can afford a new flat-screen TV because of a bonus that should be hitting our account next week. Or we might look at taking a new job and plan to take the extra pay we earn and apply it to debt. Both of these seem like reasonable decisions. The problem is that we haven't asked the Lord. Life may not happen the way we project, which makes those thoughts lofty (thinking we know best) and speculative (based on self) because we aren't God and don't know the path He has for us until we ask Him. Life comes from being aligned with God, not just from making a good decision according to our own understanding.

. . . .

Life comes from being aligned with God, not just from making a good decision according to our own understanding.

. . . .

Before we were saved, we might have regularly used these tactics, like reasoning on our own. Proverbs 3:5–6 says, *"Trust in the* LORD *with all your heart and do not lean on your own understanding. In all your ways acknowledge Him, and He will make your paths straight."* We don't need to beat ourselves up about that. We just need to recognize that relying on our own reasoning does not lead to life. We can repent of our independence from God and come back into yieldedness to Him.

When strongholds are present in our life, they impact the way we understand and see life without God. Human reasoning is living separately from God. Strongholds help us survive when we only have our own strength to choose from. Our reasoning is only protecting the stronghold, and it covers over our weakness. That leads to hiding, deceiving ourselves and others, and constricting what we can and cannot be and do. We're powerless, and most importantly, we're not communing with God. That's why we end up explaining away situations instead of owning up to them.

It's why we blame others or ourselves. It's why there's a way that seems right, but it leads to death (separation from God). We have these hoops we jump through to try to keep that sense of shame from lack covered over because it feels bad.

Generational Strongholds

Strongholds can be generational as well. I mean this in two ways: naturally and spiritually. Learned value systems or behavioral patterns can be acquired from parents, grandparents, and on up a generational line. However, because strongholds take on a supernatural (spiritual) quality, they can also be passed on spiritually. That means that even if you never came into contact with one of the family members in your generational line, some of their agreements with the Enemy can still affect you. That may seem hard to believe, but I have seen the Lord tear down agreements in many people's lives that their ancestors made and were manifesting in the present. Do not be alarmed by this. The Lord is faithful to reveal those agreements to you if they are affecting you.

Maybe you are wondering if you have any strongholds. Maybe you are worried about how many you have. We all have them; it is the nature of being human and living with a fallen nature. In the next section, we'll look at indicators that point to the presence of a stronghold in your life. But first, let me share a little more about Mark and his Exchange experience.

My Exchange took me to the place where I first made an agreement with the poverty mind-set. I was reminded of a time when I was working hard in the garden with one of my uncles. It was a hot summer day, and I just kept physically pushing myself. I would not take a break because I saw needing a break as weakness. I thought it was complaining if I needed to stop, and I would not talk with others because I thought it was a distraction. I just pressed on because I thought that was the right move. I believed the lie that people only want someone who will keep silent and just work, work, work. I also believed the lie that people only respect someone if they have that kind of work ethic. I told myself, *You will only get ahead in life if you adopt that mind-set.*

Now, listen to what Mark says the Lord showed him.

In the Exchange, Jesus showed me that was not what He wanted for my life. He showed me that He was in the garden with me and my uncle harvesting the vegetables. He did not mind me working, but He wanted me to enjoy myself and not be a slave to the process or agree with something He did not have planned for my life. He gave me a voice for a reason, and He does not want others to take advantage of a good work ethic. He also showed me that my mother was the way she was, not because of a strong ethic but because she had cowered down to the abuses of life. She, too, was not walking in liberty. He showed me how so many of my decisions in life were based on that one principle that *He never told me to believe.* I settled so many times. As a result, I allowed many people to take advantage of me over time. I co-signed for people, I accepted lesser jobs, I settled for lesser gifts than what the Father originally wanted to give to me, I entered a marriage I should not have become part of, and I put handcuffs on myself throughout life (emphasis added).

The existence of a false mind-set kept the revelation of Jesus out of Mark's life. Over time, he had adopted the stronghold he saw in his own mother and built brick upon brick of choices and lies that upheld that idea—*Don't be weak. Don't ask for things. Don't stop working. Keep silent.*

Red-Light Indicators of Strongholds

I have been in ministry for forty-two years. I have come to know the Lord in amazing and deep ways. I've experienced difficult times and fulfilling times. Interestingly, it has been in the difficult places that I've had the deepest fellowship with Him. Those times of brokenness and humility have given me opportunity to come out of "stuck places" (the approval of people, loneliness, fear of failure) more than the easier times.

Living an Exchanged life is the only way for true satisfaction. Strongholds keep us from living this life, but they are also the red-light indicators on our life dashboard alerting us of a problem that needs to be addressed. In that way, they represent the kindness of God drawing us and leading us to repentance, to come back into dependence and communion with Him. When you see your "stuck places" this way, they become redemptive pathways to the fullness of God instead of obstacles that trigger fear, shame, and destructive coping patterns.

I'll share a personal story as an example of what that looks like. I withdrew a lot when I was a kid. My childhood home had a lot of conflict—tension, anger, and unresolved issues.

I was a sensitive child, so I would go to my room, play cards, and rant and rave about everyone. I was building brick upon brick of bitterness, anger, and judgments through what I would repeat in my mind and out loud. This self-dialogue trapped me into staying withdrawn. I thought, *They won't even let me talk; they talk over me all the time; my heart doesn't count.* These excuses convinced me to just keep withdrawing.

Arguments were never reconciled in my family. Everyone just went to their separate rooms, and the next day, we all acted like everything was hunky-dory. I'd built up anger and bitterness, so my perception of the situation was already bent and twisted. I justified my withdrawal because it protected my anger and bitterness. Self-justification led to blame and shame toward everyone else. All these trappings came in because I was trying to balance my scales to be okay, to be able to sleep at night. Living in this environment was a huge hurdle for me.

When I was in college, the Lord put His thumb on it because I was pretty shy and insecure. He drew my attention to it because He was beginning to call me and prepare me for ministry. Being withdrawn wasn't a trait that could stay if I was in ministry.

I believe that because of the bitterness, the anger, and the junk that was in my life, I got sick during my sophomore year in college. I had to stay home all summer with my mother. In hindsight, I see that was the Lord having me lean into a pressure point.

I evidently didn't work through it all because the next summer I had to have knee surgery. I again had to stay home with my mom every day. I had a cast on my leg, so she washed my hair and helped me into the bathtub. I didn't want her to touch me at that stage of my life. I was aware that this whole withdrawal-anger reaction was a big issue I had to overcome.

During that time, I began spending more and more time in the Word, partly because I was bored and needed to pass the time and partly because I wanted to be away from my family. I'd go out on the patio and memorize whole chapters of scripture—literally. The Lord used that to radically soften my heart.

I went back to college, and one day in my apartment as I was spending time in the Word, the Lord said *Boom! Now is the time to deal with this bitterness issue.* I repented of the anger and bitterness I had chosen to gird myself with in order to survive. Those walls came down. Bitterness had crept into other relationships, but the Lord dealt with it all. The stronghold broke through repentance, and then the love of God filled those places. The power of having hidden God's Word in my heart that summer began to live in and through me. People began to tell me they saw something different in me. I had a joy and freedom that caused them to be drawn to me in a new way.

About a year later, God called me to ministry in a supernatural way. People were saying to me, even before they knew what God was doing in my heart, "I see that you're going to be working with college students." I had always been a behind-the-scenes kind of person, but I knew in order to do what God was calling me to do, I would have to change.

I wrestled with the Lord like Jacob did in Genesis 32, asking God for His blessing to be able to yield to His will. I knew that apart from being in His will I wouldn't be fulfilled. He showed me my unbelief and fear about being able to step into a calling like that. I repented and yielded to His design for my life.

These strongholds aren't humanly discerned. We can't discover the root of our strongholds based on human reasoning. No human can fix our strongholds. We can't give someone a revelation about their own strongholds until God allows them to experience the truth of what is happening inside of them. That's what Paul means when he says the weapons of our warfare aren't flesh; they're divinely powerful. These places where we're stuck must be dealt with through the power of supernatural weapons in order to demolish them.

Tearing Down Strongholds

The question now is, how do we tear down strongholds? Remember, this is about knowing God. It's about removing blocks that keep us from the knowledge of God. Psalm 27:4, 8 says, *"One thing I have asked from the LORD, that I shall seek: That I may dwell in the house of the LORD all the days of my life, to behold the beauty of the LORD and to meditate in His temple. When You said, 'Seek My face,' my heart said to You, 'Your face, O LORD, I shall seek.'"*

This is a posture of asking the Lord questions and listening for His responses. This is the dynamic we have in tearing down a stronghold because usually we don't even understand how it got built in our life. We need to relate to the deep love of God and His amazing ability to supply what we don't know or understand. Meditating on the Word of God in the areas of our need helps build our faith to believe He will do what He says. When I meditate on scripture, I like to use a dictionary to expand the meaning of key words. That increases my faith to see even greater depths of who God is and what He promises us.

. . . .

Meditating on the Word of God in the areas of our need helps build our faith to believe He will do what He says.

. . . .

This takes time. It is tempting as American Christians to move at the same pace as our society moves, which is immediately. If things don't come quickly, we often grow impatient and move on. We also are a conference society that loves hearing rich teachings from great speakers who have paid a heavy price to gain the intimacy and confidence they have in God, but we don't want to pay the same price to have that kind of walk with God ourselves. Paul said in Philippians 3 that he counted all things as loss in view of the surpassing value of knowing Christ his Lord. He was even willing to be put in jail for his faith in order to know God. We must take time to be with the Lord so He can show us great and mighty truths we do not know. This is key to taking down strongholds.

We get to come before the throne of God and ask Him, "What is this, and how did it get here?" We are engaging the Spirit of God in our spirit so we can gain understanding about the root of our pain. The first step is to come into the presence of God humbly and thank Him that He knows you and that He wants to set you free. Then set your mind on Him and His ability to unravel the structures set against your life to harm you. For you to understand what has been blocking you, God must give you revelation so you can know what He knows happened to you that laid the foundation for the stronghold. Revelation from God brings confidence that what He reveals, He wants to heal. Once you know your need, it's helpful to remember your position in the heavenlies so you can see what your position there gives you access to in contrast to where you currently are in your "stuck place."

For instance, if your "stuck place" has to do with rejection and the Lord shows you in your Exchange that it came from feeling alone and not being heard or valued in your family, then you can ask the Lord to show you what is true in heaven. You will realize by the Spirit that in heaven, you have been totally accepted by God and that He lavishes His love on you. When you know this, you begin to take down the bricks of your feelings and thoughts that have held up the structure of rejection in you, and you can move through forgiveness with true compassion toward those who have hurt you.

You are hurting because of rejection from your family, and yet you know to some degree what God says about you in heaven. But your emotions and mind-set don't line up. Here's where we begin to tear down the wall. We ask the Lord to show us all the lies we have believed in key experiences that have held us captive to the Enemy and our soul. As the Lord begins to take us back into our past and bring up specific situations, ask Him, "What did I believe because of that?"

By faith, we get to go into the situation that hurt us and forgive each person who impacted us in a rejecting way. We then must repent and renounce the lie we agreed with that established a stronghold. We also must forgive those who we felt mistreated us. We repent for agreeing with the specific stronghold, allowing it to occupy our soul. In this case, we would repent for agreeing with rejection itself. It's helpful to literally tell the stronghold, "I don't want to agree with you anymore. I choose to break ties with you. I tell you to get out of my life *now*."

Then you ask the Holy Spirit to fill that place so Jesus Christ can be Lord there now. As a side note, when a person gives their life to Christ and receives the infilling of the Spirit (Eph. 5:18; Acts 19:4–6), the power of the Spirit doesn't have room to flow through that person where another spirit is occupying that space. So after pulling down a stronghold, you always want to ask the Spirit to fill what has been cleaned out. We don't want to leave any ground the Enemy can come back and build on again.

This time with God is very personal. We get to be ourselves. We have been experiencing hurt, disappointment, and fear. We get to be human with the Lord in this intimate space, calling on Him and asking questions that relate to our pain. We are asking with the deep desire to discover the problem and then be able to work through it and get freedom in its place. It's good to take notes so you can continue relating with God over what He has shown you. He may show you even more things you need to pray through, or He may expand and deepen your healing.

Here's a note of encouragement. If you have a fear of failing in being intimate with God in these ways and others, I want to reassure you that He is the safest person I know. He knows you better than anyone and has loved you completely. You cannot fail with God because He is the fullness, not us. You get to receive the unconditional love of God because of *His* ability to love, not yours. He doesn't have an expectation for you to perform in the secret place with Him, so it is impossible to fail. If this is how you feel, I've written a prayer at the end of this chapter for you to speak over yourself and to the Lord, releasing those feelings to Him and inviting His full justification and love for you to fill you.

Spiritual Weapons

I want us to take a closer look at one section in 2 Corinthians.

For though we walk in the flesh, we do not war according to the flesh, for the weapons of our warfare are not of the flesh, but divinely powerful for the destruction of fortresses. We are destroying speculations and every lofty thing raised up against the knowledge of God, and we are taking every thought captive to the obedience of Christ, and we are ready to punish all disobedience, whenever your obedience is complete.

—2 Cor. 10:3–6

Our strongholds are spiritual structures. In order to tear down a spiritual structure, we need spiritual weapons. We have four key weapons at our disposal that will destroy our strongholds: repentance, forgiveness, yieldedness, and faith through obedience. Let's look at each of these.

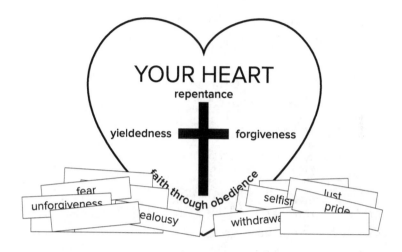

Repentance

Repentance begins with becoming aware of the lies we believed throughout our life. We need supernatural exposure to the lie and supernatural exposure to the truth. God is the One who reveals this to us, and He is the One who directs us. It may help to ask the Spirit to show you how to be seated directly in front of God's throne in heaven.

When we believe something that doesn't line up with God, our response is to repent, which means to change our mind. We can humbly tell the Holy Spirit, "I'm not in touch with all my issues. I see behavioral patterns, but I'm asking You to give me revelation of why those patterns are influencing my life." Then we listen, write down what we hear, and make a list. When we get revelation of the patterns that have affected us, we are able to repent and come out of agreement with them.

What are the weapons of repentance? They are the blood of Christ, the power of His Word, agreeing with His Word, and the truth that you have His righteousness. Those are all weapons for me. So I bring my sin, or unaligned beliefs, to God.

What does repentance look like? It actually has two parts:

1. Remorse over what we did

2. Changing the direction our lives are headed

Sometimes people think, *Well, I'm just going to change what I think about it*. But they haven't dealt with their emotions or their will to come into agreement. Our soul is a three-strand cord: mind, will, and emotions. We change our thinking to agree with God; we yield our emotions to have His Spirit fill us; and we submit our will in obedience to Him.

Repentance gives us a new heart, like it says in Ezekiel 36:26. It isn't a hard heart anymore. It is a soft, moldable, pliable heart. Make a statement to realign your will with God's will. It may sound something like this: *Lord, where my will has been in alignment with the sin in my members, I renounce (name it), and I choose to align my will with spirit and life*. This is a necessary step in changing the direction of your life and getting realigned with the Lord.

Forgiveness

Throughout the process of tearing down a stronghold, there are always people involved in the pain of our "stuck place." We must forgive them for their lack of ability to love and provide our need the way we felt they should have. Most people are stuck in some way that keeps them from loving others well. To be honest, there are many times that we fail others, intentionally and unintentionally. We want others to forgive us, so we should forgive others as well. The number one cause of sickness of every kind is unforgiveness. You will read in Chapter 7 the tremendous power of forgiveness in our lives.

It was a great revelation when I realized my parents were really just people and I could actually forgive them for not having it all together. It wasn't their fault that they didn't nurture me in ways I wish they would have, and I could see now how all the other things they did were amazing. Understanding this was essential to my ability to forgive and be healed. We are all sinners and fall short of the glory (the perfection) of God (Rom. 3:23). We are to love above all else, and when we have grace and mercy toward ourselves, we can extend the same to others, and vice versa. Forgiving others is one of the highest values of God because it is what He did for us.

In order to get real freedom, we have to apply the whole Word of God as we live this out. It won't be like a wand waved over us where we become healed and delivered and are now perfect in our behavior. People deceive themselves into thinking that's what should happen. We have to wrestle with the promises of God. We have to wrestle with the Word, like Jacob did with the angel until he was blessed (Gen. 32:24), until the truth comes alive in us.

Yieldedness

Yieldedness means to submit or surrender. We must take a place of submission to hear from God and respond rightly to Him. I've seen through my counseling that most "stuck places" originate before we're eight or nine years old. We are already born into independence and rebellion toward God. Our difficulty in responding to God comes from that rebellion.

Our childhood issues begin because of this independence and our reinforcement of it. In almost all Exchanges we have with God, we should repent of rebellion.

The key to freedom from strongholds is learning and deciding to surrender to the truth that God is God and I am not. At the root of every stronghold is our sin nature in control, trying to build life according to what we have determined is good and right. That whole belief structure is faulty. Our strongholds become beneficial when we allow them to lead us to humility, acknowledging that our ways do not lead to real life, eternal life. The true nature of a believer is as a bondservant—one who has decided to yield his or her life to God as master.

The good news is that He is a Master who loves us and always has our best interests. Contrary to the modern definition of slave, the Bible uses the term *bond slave* or *bondservant* to refer to someone who voluntarily serves another. To yield your life to God means you recognize God as God and choose to give your life to serve Him because He is the only One worthy. When we take this posture, it is easy to yield to God's truth as He reveals it to us throughout our journey. Being a bondservant is whole-hearted obedience to the only wise God.

I've found in Exchanges that the demonic attack that reinforced the stronghold in our youth is often connected to our purpose. The Enemy wants to capture us early so we cannot fulfill our purpose. For instance, if you were supposed to have a voice to the nations or to cities, the Enemy might try to build a stronghold that shuts down your voice so you can't fulfill your destiny. The redemptive work God does almost every time at the end of an Exchange is deeply connected to your purpose and identity.

Faith through Obedience

When we choose obedience, it punishes and defeats the disobedience that has had power in our life. When we are obedient, everything around us is brought into the freedom we're walking in. That is where we reclaim our God-given authority that Adam and Eve abdicated to the Enemy. That is how we fill the earth with God's glory.

If you decide to do an Exchange, be warned that everything in your life won't be immediately fixed. It isn't an end-all, be-all fix. It's the removal of the unbelief. It's the removal of the lie that you've believed. It's the removal of a demonic oppression in your life. Learning to walk in Christ's provision for us is a process. Overcoming the old life is not always easy, but once we make the decision to come out of agreement with lies and demonic structures, we are empowered to renew our minds every day and walk in peaceful trust in God's goodness. Now we can discover the deeper meaning of life, and we'll experience the fullness God intended for us from the beginning.

To really change requires obedience. It's not a magic pill; it's a spiritual reality that we step into agreement with. When we get free of the structure, we have power, not death, working in our lives, so we can be obedient. Now we have the power to walk in newness of life (Rom. 6:7–8).

John 14:21 (CEV) says, *"If you love me, you will do what I have said, and my Father will love you. I will also love you and show you what I am like."* The word *if* is not conditional the way we typically think of it. It's conditional in the sense that if you're a believer, you will want to obey His commandments, and then He will reveal Himself to you. The revelation of Christ increases to us through our obedience.

· · · · · · · · · · · · · · · · ·

The revelation of Christ increases to us through our obedience.

· · · · · · · · · · · · · · · ·

The foundational remedy to tearing down strongholds is humility. God is opposed to the proud, but He gives grace to the humble (James 4:6–7). As we become more in tune with God and aligning our will with His, He'll show us the areas where our thinking is misaligned where we have a wrong belief system. He is fathering us, so if we yield and stay humble, He will unlock the places in us that need to be removed so we can know Him in that area.

It takes faith to walk day by day in obedience to God. Faith isn't an emotion or even a desire. It requires action to move in response to what we know is true about God and to what He is revealing we need to do to walk in obedience. Hebrews 11:1–2 says, *"Now faith is the assurance of things hoped for, the conviction of things not seen. For by it the men of old gained approval."* This tells us that faith is the substance and is what caused the great people of God in the Word to gain His approval. James 2:26 says that faith without works has no life. So faith demonstrates our yieldedness and is necessary for obedience.

Are you wondering how things ended up for Mark? While we don't know the difficulty of the darkness Mark was living in, we do have testimony of the light that flooded his inner being after that stronghold was taken down. Listen to what he says about it now.

I broke my agreement with the lie that day. After the Exchange, I began involving Jesus in my decision-making process. I am not perfect in the process, but I am recognizing more and more that I need to include Him before deciding. When I find myself settling, either the Father will send someone my way to help me recognize, or I will hear the Holy Spirit instructing me that it is not the correct decision to make for my life. I admit that it is scary at times because it goes against a familiarity I was used to, but I'd rather do it this way first and not deal with all the negative aftermath of my wrong decision.

Mark has realized that letting the Lord lead him brings life, while living according to his own ways brings a negative aftermath, or death. That's the whole point of this chapter on strongholds, to demonstrate the goodness and trustworthiness of Christ and that when we cling to our man-made ways of protecting our heart, it will never bring the life we crave. That life can only be found in a yielded, intimate relationship with Christ.

Strongholds manifest as repeated patterns of behavior that result in "stuck places"—areas of disordered thinking that have become walled off and resistant to truth. You become stuck inside the walls you built.

Strongholds block out the light of God's truth and hold us back from the intimacy we really want. Even if it is one brick at a time, we must bring the walls down. To bring down the walls of our strongholds, we need to undo the lies (our own values, justice systems, and coping mechanisms) in order to get our hearts unstuck from the old pattern of belief and bring our thoughts into alignment with His truth. This is the dialogue we have with the Lord in an Exchange because it is in Christ that we have the power and provision to overcome our strongholds so we can walk in the fullness we had before the Fall.

Once we see the goodness of God in providing His Son and the way to live in Him, we will see how every situation from our past can be healed and restored to His fullness. This restoration will enable us to live our lives in oneness with our Father, producing freedom and the knowledge of Him. This is living the Exchanged life. His ways are higher than our ways. They are life giving!

Personal Processing

Meditate on These Verses

For though we walk in the flesh, we do not war according to the flesh, for the weapons of our warfare are not of the flesh, but divinely powerful for the destruction of fortresses. We are destroying speculations and every lofty thing raised up against the knowledge of God, and we are taking every thought captive to the obedience of Christ, and we are ready to punish all disobedience, whenever your obedience is complete.

—2 Cor. 10:3–6

Trust in the LORD with all your heart and do not lean on your own understanding. In all your ways acknowledge Him, and He will make your paths straight.

—Prov. 3:5–6

But He gives a greater grace. Therefore it says, "GOD IS OPPOSED TO THE PROUD, BUT GIVES GRACE TO THE HUMBLE." Submit therefore to God. Resist the devil and he will flee from you. Draw near to God and He will draw near to you. Cleanse your hands, you sinners; and purify your hearts, you double-minded.

—James 4:6–8

1. Sit with the Lord, and ask Him to reveal patterns in your life that do not produce life. Look at each one. Ask the Lord to show you why it's there. Give the Spirit time to reveal all He wants. You may need to keep asking questions in response to what you hear in order to get full clarity. When the Lord reveals a place in your heart that doesn't align with His truth, repent out loud, breaking your alignment with all the Enemy's lies. Ask the Lord to cleanse you with the blood of Christ, which cleanses your conscience from dead works (Heb. 9:14), and submit that area of your life back to the Lordship of Christ. Forgive those who were part of this stronghold being built in your life.

2. Speak the truth of who you are in accordance with God's Word and what He reveals in your Exchange. He always wants to show you a redemptive picture of how He sees you. Look for scriptures to build your faith. You will need to look up key words in a concordance to find scriptures that relate.

3. What are you willing to change in your life so you get enough time with the Lord to get His revelation about the places you're stuck?

4. Begin a spiritual journal (if you don't already have one), and start dialoguing with God. Use this as a space to ask Him questions. Our prayer life isn't a one-way conversation.

Prayer

Declare this out loud.

Thanks be to God, because Jesus Christ our Lord is going to rescue me from this body of death. I will overcome because I'm a child of God. I have the Spirit of Sonship inside of me; I want what You want. Thank You that the same God who raised Jesus from the dead lives in me, so You're going to raise me from the dead in places where I've been stuck and defeated. You're an overcomer, so I'm an overcomer. And I don't have to be afraid of messing up because You already made provision for that too. There is no way in Christ I can lose except by depending on myself. Thank You, thank You, thank You, thank You, Lord! Amen.

Chapter 6

SOVEREIGNTY

And we know that God causes all things to work together for good to those who love God, to those who are called according to His purpose. For those whom He foreknew, He also predestined to become conformed to the image of His Son, so that He would be the firstborn among many brethren; and these whom He predestined, He also called; and these whom He called, He also justified; and these whom He justified, He also glorified.

—Rom. 8:28–30

Let's draw back and take a bird's-eye view of the concepts we've covered to see how they're building on each other. We began by talking about how God created us to be in His family. He made us in His image and likeness. Like Him, we were made for relationship. God made us to be dependent on Him. Adam and Eve, instead of trusting God, entertained the voice of the serpent and ate from the Tree of the Knowledge of Good and Evil. Mankind tried to be like

God, without God. However, God provided a way for us to be restored to His original intent by sending His Son, Jesus, to die for our sin.

Residue of our fallen nature affects our communion with God. This residue manifests in degrading passions, drawing from self-strength, disobeying, and relying on coping mechanisms of blame and shame that keep us always trying to balance our scales so we can feel okay with ourselves. God provided the Law—religious rules—so we could be led to our need for Jesus. Jesus brought a new way, one that sets us free from the law of sin and death. Because of Jesus's sacrifice, we can be redeemed from the curse of the Law. There are no more scales to balance. There is, though, the need to learn how to live a life of communion with and dependence on God.

We are made of body, soul, and spirit. As believers, God is alive inside our spirit. When we live from the inside out, God's grace empowers us to choose to yield our body and soul to our spirit where He can commune with us. We live a life of exchanging the lies we've believed about God, ourselves, others, and the world for the truths of God. As Christians, we are simultaneously citizens of two worlds—heaven and earth. By accessing the truth and power of God, we become a conduit for heaven to invade the world, bringing God's life to mankind.

After a lifetime of using worldly coping strategies, most of us have built up strongholds that are manifested in repeated patterns of behavior and result in "stuck places." But God has given us supernatural weapons to defeat these strongholds, including repentance, submission, and forgiveness, making the way for us not to lean on our own understanding but to lean into God who knows and is the way, the truth, and the life.

That brings us to where we are now. In this chapter, we'll look at what scripture tells us about God's core characteristics—His nature and His ways. We will see how God's true character can overcome and heal every situation we find ourselves in or have been affected by. We will learn about how His commitment to work all things together for good can be apprehended as we bring all of life's situations before His throne.

God Is Always Good

Here's a mind-blowing truth you might not have heard or realized before. God's disposition is always kind, benevolent, and for our good. God is always working to position us, His children, in such a way as to lavish His unconditional love on us so we can receive it. Do you believe this? What if things don't go your way? What if circumstances don't feel good? As humans, we are temporal, or time-based, but God longs for us to develop an eternal view of our situations. Allow the Lord to take you up above and look at your life from a heavenly perspective. We want to understand the why of situations so we can have quick fixes, but we need to see what God sees in our circumstances so we can rightly align with Him, know His love for us in all things, and have true authority over our lives.

. . . .

God's disposition is always kind, benevolent, and for our good.

. . . .

God is training us to rule and reign over the earth in union with Him, but we are so focused on the temporary that we

149

miss what's really going on and the privilege of being with Him in our life circumstances. We frustrate ourselves because we're asking the wrong questions or we're not talking all the way through the issue to know His heart and mind. We need to say things like this: "I believe You are good, Lord, so what really happened here? What does it mean? What do I do next? How do You feel about me in this? Show me what that looks like here."

When we hear something from the Lord and interpret what we think it means instead of asking Him more questions, we can come to the wrong conclusions and responses. If a situation turns out differently than what He said, we could be disappointed because we didn't continue to ask what He meant. It's important in our relationship with God that we don't presume to know right away what He means.

We always need to ask until we get to the bottom line. For example, if you heard the Lord promise you provision for something but money didn't come in, you may feel like He didn't fulfill His promise. It may be that He was speaking of a different kind or source of provision. It may be that He meant it in a different timing. We can miss those details sometimes and then naturally harden our hearts out of disappointment or feelings of betrayal.

Once we have a clear understanding of what God is doing and saying, which could take several conversations over time, we can put our faith in that and move forward in peace and confidence. It's all about knowing Him . . . not just getting better. Matthew 6:33 says, *"But seek first His kingdom and His righteousness, and all these things will be added to you."* We seek Him first as the One who keeps His promises; we're not primarily seeking the promise.

. . . .

It's all about knowing Him . . . not just getting better.

. . . .

When we harden our hearts through misunderstanding Him, we reject Him as Lord of our lives. That is why it's so important to pay attention to how we position our hearts toward God. If we're mad at Him, that's okay. We can talk to Him about it until it's worked out, but we shouldn't withdraw our presence when we're mad because things aren't working out the way we think they should. Imagine if we did that with our spouses, children, or family members. Nothing would get resolved, and the relationship would stay fractured. We need to keep dialoguing until peace comes.

God is a God of unity, peace, and wholeness. Some sectors of the Christian church believe God values teaching us above loving us. I hear people say, "Well, God must have needed to teach me something, so He allowed this difficult or terrible event to happen." God does not bring bad situations into our lives. He does not punish us based on our behavior. He is redemptive. The fallenness of the world and the Devil are what bring bad times into our lives. Believing that a good God is hurting us so we can receive His love is not biblical and taints the way we view who He is and what we are worth. Thinking of God this way does not create trust or a desire to have deep intimacy with Him. We must believe according to the Word that His lovingkindness is always toward us, that His mercies are new every day, and that His grace is always available.

. . . .

Believing that a good God is hurting us so we can receive His love is not biblical and taints the way we view who He is and what we are worth.

. . . .

Many Christians spend the majority of their lives wrestling with God about life not going the way they think it should. They have yet to really know Him and haven't been able to experience His true heart toward them. As a result, they miss out on experiencing the deep love He wants to give them, all because they think they have a better plan for how their life should go.

We don't have to understand why things happen the way they do. It isn't useful to even try. Our response is to believe in His goodness despite not knowing why. Our conversation with God should sound something like this: "I don't understand why it had to happen that way, Lord, but I'm going to stop resisting You and choose to believe that You are positioning me and all of this so I can receive Your love." In Acts 17:26–27 it says that God has set us in boundaries that we would grope for Him and find Him. Through our life situations, God longs for us to pursue Him, to meet us with His love.

God knows better than we do. His ways are higher than ours—they're better than ours. Psalm 139 says His thoughts are toward us all the time. We have to work out our belief systems to agree with His Word or else our theology will be bent, which breaks our intimacy with Him. Don't let anything rob you of intimacy with God.

Discovering God's Intentions

The first chapter of Ephesians describes God's amazing intentions toward us.

> *Blessed be the God and Father of our Lord Jesus Christ, who has blessed us with every spiritual blessing in the heavenly places in Christ, just as He chose us in Him before the foundation of the world, that we would be holy and blameless before Him.* **In love He predestined us to adoption as sons through Jesus Christ to Himself, according to the kind intention of His will** (emphasis added).
>
> —Eph. 1:3–5

Think back to early in the book when I described Adam and Eve's life in the Garden of Eden. Even before the Fall, God had a plan to restore us, to bring us back into adoption as His children, His heirs. This passage is for those who believe in Jesus—He predetermined that those who choose to yield their life to Him will become His sons and daughters, inheriting all the blessings of heaven, the riches of His glory, and the forgiveness of sin, and become holy and blameless before Him. He is committed to finishing His purpose for us. When we say yes to Him, we receive everything He had in store for us; we receive what He decided He would be to us and what that would give us access to—all of heaven.

> *[T]o the praise of the glory of His grace, which He freely bestowed on us in the Beloved.* **In Him we have redemption through His blood,** *the forgiveness of our*

trespasses, according to the riches of His grace which He lavished on us (emphasis added).

—Eph. 1:6–8

God redeemed us through the blood of Christ. Why was it His blood that redeemed us? His blood carries God-life that seals the covenant between God and man; it transfers that life, the life of God, to His children. God's blood is untainted and flawless; it has no guilt, no jealousy. His blood cleanses our consciences. The Enemy cannot overcome the blood of Jesus Christ.

In the book *The Power of the Blood of Jesus*, Andrew Murray writes, "The hidden value of His blood is the spirit of self-sacrifice, and where the blood really touches the heart, it works out in that heart, a like spirit of self-sacrifice. We learn to give up ourselves and our lives, so as to press into the full power of that new life, which the blood has provided."[3]

When we speak the blood of Jesus over something, it transforms the situation because the blood of Christ is the key to life. There can be no life apart from the blood.

Christ also lavished on us the riches of His grace. The word *lavish* calls to mind the image of a cascading coverage of grace over us. What is grace? It is His supernatural empowerment to us and in us. The riches of His supernatural empowerment means there is no end to its supply or its ability to do what it is sent to do.

---

3. Andrew Murray, *The Power of the Blood of Jesus* (Abbotsford: Aneko Press, 2017), 14.

GRACE

The free and unmerited favor of God as manifested in the salvation of sinners and the bestowal of blessings; undeserved favor, the fullness of God.

The term *grace* is often misused. People say, "Hey, I messed up. Give me grace." Humans can't give grace. We've interchanged that word with *mercy*. Mistakes warrant mercy from one another, which is the covering and release of lack or fault with love. Grace can only come from God, which is the supernatural empowerment of God to do in us and through us what we cannot do for ourselves. God empowers us to love, to be sanctified, and even to choose Him. It's not about striving, self-strength, or performing. It's about resting in the measure of His grace that is poured out lavishly. There's no end.

*He made known to us **the mystery of His will**, according to His kind intention which He purposed in Him with a view to an administration suitable to the fullness of the times, that is, the summing up of all things in Christ, things in the heavens and things on the earth"* (emphasis added).

—Eph. 1:9–10

God's intentions for us are kind. God revealed His mysterious plan to us. The mystery of His will is that all things are in Christ, to Christ, and through Christ. God's plan from the beginning was for us to have communion with Him. Christ is the mystery of how that happens. Because God made

155

it possible for us to be reconciled through the price Christ paid on the cross and through His resurrection, we are now positioned fully in Christ and have been given the Holy Spirit as a seal. All the promises of God are yes in Christ, and our part is to bring our mind, will, and emotions into agreement. All these promises are ours because of the promise of the Holy Spirit. Christ's blood flows in us.

> [A]lso we have **obtained an inheritance,** having been predestined according to His purpose who works all things after the counsel of His will, to the end that we who were the first to hope in the Christ would be to the praise of His glory. In Him, you also, after listening to the message of truth, the gospel of your salvation—having also believed, you were sealed in Him with the Holy Spirit of promise, who is given as a pledge of our inheritance, with a view to the redemption of God's own possession, to the praise of His glory (emphasis added).
>
> —Eph. 1:11–14

Our inheritance is that now, as believers, we have been predetermined (predestined) by God to be conformed to the fullness of Christ. He sealed us in the Holy Spirit, which means that all His power and might to do good for us and in us will be fulfilled. All His promises are available to us to restore everything that was lost through the Fall. The highest treasure and blessing of all—complete oneness with Him—is now our promised reward.

Knowing this is the truth about God, we can see that all the times we've judged God or been offended by God were based on our own fallen understanding. In our humanity, we measure God according to our circumstances, viewing life based on our experiences. When we don't know God, we don't understand His ways. We draw conclusions from our experiences, our pains, and our disappointments, and we decide that's how life works. When we do this, we are setting ourselves up as judge and king of our own systems. That is one reason we see so many value systems raging against each other on earth. Remember, the Word says that every one of us has turned aside from God. None of us are worthy to judge Him. Psalm 53:2–3 says, *"God has looked down from heaven upon the sons of men to see if there is anyone who understands, who seeks after God. Every one of them has turned aside; together they have become corrupt; there is no one who does good, not even one."*

God wants to be kind and good to us all the time. Even in challenging life circumstances, God is positioning us to grope for Him, to discover truth and life so we can be free. It's the fallen world that brings difficulties into our lives. Our circumstances are meant to humble us and lead us to Christ as our only source for true life (Acts 17:26–28).

God Will Not Violate His Own Character or His Created Order

In Genesis, we read that God created the world, and at each stage, He called it good. When God made mankind, He called it very good. That's why He could hand over the earth to mankind to rule over and propagate it. God will never violate that.

Many people are mad at God because He did this or didn't do that, but He gave the earth to us. That doesn't mean God gave us the earth to rule and reign over and then left us to ourselves while He watched from afar. He didn't say,

"Well, you're on your own." Far from it! We are to co-labor with Him. Whenever we do not invite Him in, we suffer the consequences of our choices. Remember, God created us in His image where fullness of life only comes through abiding communion with Him, and a life lived independently from Him leads to death (Deut. 30).

. . . .

**Whenever we do not invite Him in,
we suffer the consequences
of our choices.**

. . . .

Even when we have chosen independence, God has an eternal way for it all to be redeemed. Through repentance, we can always turn back to God, and He will restore us to our original place in Him and with Him because He is kind and long-suffering.

It is in His order that mankind has responsibility over the earth. That is why we witness good and evil taking place here. Man is created in God's image, but because of sin, our fallen nature impacts the way we rule until His divine nature in us overcomes our soulish nature. Many people have their own agendas and manifest whatever is necessary to accomplish that agenda. If God is in charge of their agenda, He is revealed. If man's own nature is ruling, then their self-life is revealed, sin abounds, and they are prone to believe the lies the Enemy tells.

As Christians, we are called to rise up amid the chaos and strife happening around us and reveal Christ in all situations because He has given us all authority in Him. We know Him and have His heart; we are to move in His ways and release Him every day. God has given us as His sons and daughters the authority to speak things in the spirit realm for the purpose of reconciling things on earth to heaven.

This is His order: God in man, ruling on earth.

The Working Order of Life

Let me tell you a powerful story that will exhibit the overarching truths of this chapter. While I was working at the Baptist University around 1996, the community experienced a tragedy that set the stage for the truths you're reading in this chapter.

It was Mother's Day weekend. Two cars with five amazing students headed home to Kansas City to be with their moms. When they were on their way back to school and about forty minutes away, the driver and passengers of the lead car fell asleep while the car was going up a hill. The car veered into the oncoming lane. A large tractor trailer truck was coming over the hill in the opposite direction and picking up speed. Unable to see the students' car veer into his lane, the truck driver plowed into them, killing everyone in that car and the car behind them.

The university asked me to attend the visitation services for two of the students. The families were all Christians and loved the Lord. While I was there, I heard statements such as, "Well, I guess the Lord needed them in heaven more than we needed them here" and "The Devil took them out too soon." This was so grievous to me because I thought, *How will the families ever recover if that is what they believe?* It led me to the truths of this chapter in a clearer way than I'd ever known them before.

Let's start by looking at how the Lord has set up the universe. First, we should define the word *sovereignty*. It is the supremacy of God, the kingship of God; He is the One who ultimately rules over the order of all things and its established end. He works all things together according to His will, causing mankind's free will and the enemy's schemes to submit to His eternal redemptive plans and purposes. As we have already discussed, He chose to give mankind rulership over the earth under His stewardship and through submission to His will and way.

Now let's factor in another piece to this dynamic—Satan. Before the world was formed, Satan (or Lucifer) was a high-ranking angel. He was an angelic cherub created in heaven to worship God, but his heart was proud. Satan chose to rebel against God, and he and a horde of angels who chose to follow him were cast out of heaven (Ezek. 28; Isa. 14). When Adam and Eve chose to agree with the serpent (Satan) in the garden and reject the voice (will) of God, they set rebellion in motion in their lives as well. In Ephesians 2, we see that when this happened, God determined for a time that Satan (the prince of the power of the air) would be allowed to work in the lives of the sons of disobedience—all humanity. Because of mankind's choice to follow Satan, God had to set another plan in place to make it possible for humans to be restored to God's original intent.

Because God is God, He already knew what humans would choose, but because of His love for us, He gave us free will to make those choices. Love isn't love without freedom to choose. Our complete journey on earth is the love of God longing to have intimate friendship with those He created while giving them the freedom to choose. Through His sovereignty, He is always giving us opportunities to choose.

He is constantly wooing us toward His love, longing for us to choose His ways so we can come back to His sovereign goodness toward us.

. . . .

Our complete journey on earth is the love of God longing to have intimate friendship with those He created while giving them the freedom to choose.

. . . .

When we do not choose to come into His ways, His wrath is toward the unrighteousness we are agreeing with. We experience His anger against sin whenever we engage in the Enemy's death structure. God is a righteous God and must punish all that is unrighteous (the works of the Enemy). I John 3:8 (NLT) says, "*But when people keep on sinning, it shows that they belong to the devil, who has been sinning since the beginning. But the Son of God came to destroy the works of the devil.*"

Sometimes our circumstances feel hard, but that struggle is for our good. The Israelites left Egypt and wandered in the wilderness for forty years. That entire experience showed them what was in their hearts, and God used that time to get the Egypt out of them, to rid them of a slave mind-set so they could come into true worship and receive the blessing their Father had for them. Wilderness seasons discipline and train you for the life He has for you.

God is sovereign over all. For a time, the Enemy has the ability to rule over the power of the air to harass and test the human heart. We have a choice whom we will follow.

God's sovereignty means He is *able* to work out the kind intention of His will and work all things for our good.

In the same way the Spirit also helps our weakness; for we do not know how to pray as we should, but the Spirit Himself intercedes for us with groanings too deep for words; and He who searches the hearts knows the mind of the Spirit is, because He intercedes for the saints according to the will of God. And we know that God causes all things to work together for good to those who love God, to those who are called according to His purpose.

—Rom. 8:26–28

Let's look again at the story of the college students. First, God loves His children and does not bring harm to them. It is not His good pleasure to take them away from their loved ones. Second, the Devil can indeed have an impact on our lives, but he cannot take people out on his own before God's ordained days are finished (Ps. 139:16). So what other factors are involved when these kinds of situations happen?

If we do not have the full understanding of everything that affects our lives, we will not be able to fully reconcile our life experiences to God's order and kind intentions toward us. Even as believers, we tend to bring God down to our circumstances. We are supposed to be learning how to bring our circumstances into alignment with what God promises in His Word. This is the maturing process of every believer. We must take captive every thought to obey what God says is true.

Living Out This Reality

Because of the Fall, we are now subjected to five influencing factors on earth.

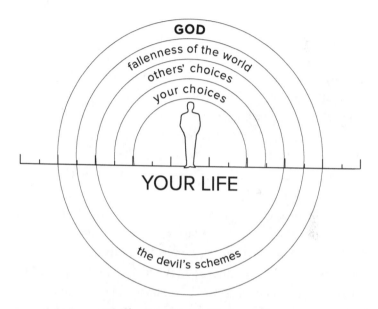

The Sovereignty Diagram

1. Your Choices
2. Others' Choices
3. Fallenness of the World
4. The Devil's Schemes
5. God's Sovereignty

To correctly diagnose our point of pain and take the appropriate biblical action, we must identify the factors responsible for our pain. Am I hurt because of my own poor choices? Did someone else make a choice that affected me? Maybe the pain was caused by the fallen world we live in that is rife with sin. Sometimes it truly is the influence of the Enemy. It could be any combination of that list.

In our daily lives, we constantly encounter situations that apart from God we are ill-equipped to succeed in. According to Ephesians 1:17–19, the Lord wants to give us wisdom and revelation in the knowledge of Him, the hope of His calling for us, the riches of His inheritance in us, and the ability to walk in the surpassing greatness of His power daily. That's amazing! As we go about our daily lives, we have access at all times to these truths to cause our lives to be great. We just have to learn how to process our situations all the way through with Him.

Before Christ came into our lives, we regularly misidentified the source of pain in our situations. We typically could only do that by what was visible to us in the natural realm, which didn't always fully account for all the factors that impacted the situation. As unbelievers, we didn't have the spiritual capacity to discern or rectify our emotions, much less recognize the impact the demonic realm might be having on our being. When we aren't able to identify correctly and fully all that has affected us, we misplace our emotional, mental, and physical responses. Remember the chapter on strongholds? God wants regular, deep conversation with us to take us past our own understanding and reveal to us what is blocking our journey with Him. We have to choose to make time for this level of relating.

The more we misidentify the source of our pain, the more we get trapped in shame and blame, building broken belief systems that continue to shape our future choices. We are responsible for our own choices—all of them. Even if we think other people or the warfare around us pressed us into those choices, we are still responsible for how we choose to respond. When we feel pressed by others' choices, the Enemy's attacks, or what is happening around us, we still have the responsibility and ability to find God and choose His ways in order to overcome.

I want to clarify something about Satan's influence and spiritual warfare. I mentioned earlier that spiritual warfare can occur because of an open door in our life. It can also occur as a result of an internal or external pressure, although not necessarily because we've already agreed with the Enemy. When Jesus was tempted by Satan in the wilderness, He had been fasting for forty days. He may have been tired, and we know He was hungry. Each time the Enemy taunted Him, Jesus chose the truth of God to combat him.

In the Garden of Gethsemane, Jesus was in a tremendous battle with the will of God. In His humanity, Jesus felt the weight of the call to go all the way to the cross, which would pay the price for the redemption of mankind. Hebrews 12:1–4 lets us see into the price Christ paid on that journey of decision-making in the garden. This was an internal battle of laying down His life to fulfill the will of God. The Bible says that subduing His will and resisting the Enemy was so intense that He sweat drops of blood. There is a heavy cost to following God and fulfilling His will.

Sometimes the warfare comes from the outside. For example, Shadrach, Meshach, and Abed-nego, who refused to bow down to other gods, were thrown into a furnace of fire and continued to worship God despite all the pressure.

Shadrach, Meshach and Abed-nego replied to the king, "O Nebuchadnezzar, we do not need to give you an answer concerning this matter. If it be so, our God whom we serve is able to deliver us from the furnace of blazing fire; and He will deliver us out of your hand, O king. But even if He does not, let it be known to you, O king, that we are not going to serve your gods or worship the golden image that you have set up."

—Dan. 3:16–18

This is how someone responds who has set his or her heart and mind on God no matter what others say.

To get free from broken theology and cycles, we must reconcile our perceptions with the truth of God's character and ways. We cannot decide who God is by what our value system says He should be or do. We are to know who He is and how His ways work. That takes time with Him and in His Word. God trumps our value system, which is primarily built on what we think protects and prospers us the most from a worldly perspective. His ways are higher than our ways, and His thoughts are higher than our thoughts (Isa. 55:8–9). Remember, it takes spiritual weapons to take down spiritual realities—and *everything* is spiritual.

How do we know what impacts us? We ask God.

In order to work through the five influences that affect our lives each day, especially related to painful events, we must know the biblical response that will bring healing. Here are the biblical actions that correspond to each of the five influences in our daily life.

1. **Your Choices** – When we make a choice that doesn't align with God, we must repent in order to have freedom in our spirit and soul. If we do not take ownership of our own sin, we are bound

166

in that sin and will suffer the repercussions of that sin.

2. **Others' Choices** – When others sin against us, the Word tells us to forgive. We will talk more about forgiveness in the next chapter.

3. **Fallenness of the World** – This includes premature death, sickness, disasters, and tiredness. The Lord has given us authority over the fallenness of this world, but for us to exercise it, we must first be sure we are submitted to God and then ask Him what He is doing and how He would have us take authority. This influencing factor is mostly overlooked in the way Christians resolve their situations, but it is so important in order for us to deal with it.

4. **The Devil's Schemes** – It is the Enemy's constant desire to get you to not worship God. The Word also tells us that Satan is roaring about, seeking whom he may devour. James 4:6–8 tells us that we are to humble ourselves, submit to God, and resist the Devil, and he will flee. To resist the Devil, we must not come into agreement with anything he says. It's important to know the Word of God so you can easily discern the Enemy's lies.

5. **God's Sovereignty** – Humble yourself before God and obey Him. Remember that Romans 8:28 says that God causes all things to work together for good for those who love Him. Believers are to believe that He always wants good for them. When you resist blaming Him for the hurtful things in your life, you can receive His kind intentions to

take all the other four factors and work them for good. This is submitting to God. This is living by faith.

Now let's go back to my example about the college students and work through the five influencing factors. Remember, while I was at the visitation, I heard two things that disturbed me: "God must have needed those students more than we did" and "The Enemy took them out before their time." These statements bothered me because they do not line up with the Word of God or His lovingkindness for us. They also didn't take into account the individuals involved or their fallen condition.

The first piece of information I learned was that the students had stayed up late both nights before their trip back to school. They were exhausted (fallen nature) and evidently didn't set up a plan for how they would stay awake and alert while driving. That created a weakness in them that the Enemy could have taken advantage of and set his plan in motion to take their lives. I believe this is the correct application of truth related to the choices they made.

In this situation, it would have helped those who were hurting from these kids' deaths if they could have forgiven the students for not making a plan to ensure they were awake and protected. They could also then make declarative statements to the Enemy about their loss, telling him that he will not torment their loved ones with regret and hopelessness over the situation. They could also release their grief by acknowledging these other factors so any blame they wanted to put other places could be taken away.

Working through the Five Factors

Think of a painful circumstance in your life that may have caused you to doubt God's goodness. Work through each of the five influencing factors by asking the Lord how each factor impacted the situation. Then ask the Lord more specific questions about that factor's effect and what it built up inside of you. For example, if someone else's choice caused you pain, ask the Lord what you chose to believe because of that and how you learned to cope. Invite the Lord to reveal truth in its place. Once you receive and agree with the truth, the stronghold of the Lord replaces the stronghold of the Enemy, and you can walk in freedom. Many times, pulling out the lies in one situation unravels the lies that came in through other situations and pulls it all the way out of your life. That's a miracle!

It's important that you be honest with yourself about your pain. Maybe you're whitewashing the whole picture. Acknowledge that this still hurts you even if you don't know why. Own it if you have a share in the fault of that painful situation, even if it's only a little bit.

If you can't break through something quickly, go through the five factors again to discern all that's going on beneath the surface. *What is my part? What is their part? What is the fallenness of the world?* Make regular use of this tool when you've been hurt, when you're in conflict with someone, or when a painful situation has occurred. Remember, God is redemptive over all of it. He wants to restore what was lost in your situation, your identity, and your worth.

When we are unable to invite God into a situation, it's often because we don't believe Him yet in that way. God doesn't cause everything, but as we search for Him within the boundaries of our lives where things take place, we will find Him. That is how God causes *all things* to work together for our good (Rom. 8:28).

This gives you an opportunity to dialogue with Him so you can have revelation and get to the place where you believe Him. Do the work, and dig out the revelation with God until the lightbulb comes on. Nobody can turn the lightbulb on for you. No one can do the work for you. You have to talk it through with the Lord. People can help by pointing you in a certain direction, but ultimately, you have to go to the Lord for that lightbulb to fully shine. Invite God into it. There's no shame that you don't believe Him yet.

I recommend that you have a notebook with you when you spend time with God. Keep one wherever you engage the Lord. Write down what you ask God and what you think you hear Him say. What you hear may not be the whole message He has for you, but it provides another opportunity for you to ask more questions. *Well, God, I have this job offer, and I don't have a sense one way or the other. God, what are You saying about that? What do You want me to believe about that? What do You want me to pray about that?* Just keep asking Him questions so He gives you direction about what to do with what you hear. But stop disqualifying it. Run with it. The Holy Spirit is faithful enough to let you know if it really wasn't Him.

God is talking to us a lot more than we realize. We may have a lofty idea of what God is supposed to sound like, but let me slay that myth. God lives in you, and He sounds a lot like you. If you're directing a question to Him, believe 100 percent that whatever you are hearing in response is Him if it agrees with His character and Word. I can guarantee that if it's not Him, you will know it because what you hear will be full of yourself, puffing yourself up, and self-protection, and it will result in a feeling of pressure or condemnation. That's the Enemy. It's that simple. But if you're directing your heart toward God, believe that it's Him. Trust it.

You might be tempted to ask a yes-or-no question, but I would be cautious with that because it's easy to be confused. The body of sin in your members might want to say no, and the Lord might be saying yes. If you do ask a yes-or-no question and you hear both answers, then say, "Well, Lord, I think You're the One telling me yes, but could You tell me something more about the yes? What would that look like? Keep building on it." Don't get bound up thinking, *Oh, I can't ask yes-or-no questions.* Just don't use your own thinking to figure out whether it is the Lord saying yes or your bodily members saying yes. The Lord's answers are always going to be consistent with His nature and His Word. Always.

. . . .

The Lord's answers are always going to be consistent with His nature and His Word.

. . . .

To summarize, we are primarily about knowing God and wanting to spend time in His presence. This doesn't mean we can't build, create, and dream. But He is our first priority. Spending time with Him reveals to us His nature, which is pure love and goodness. I'll say it again. He is always working to position His children so He can lavish His love on them. Our wounds do not come from the Lord, but He desperately wants to heal us.

Our wounds create "stuck places," and many of those "stuck places" are the result of not being able to forgive— forgive ourselves, forgive someone else, forgive God. But when we see God's heart desire to be good toward us and accept the tools He's given us to access His goodness, we become highly motivated to forgive, and we allow God to finally begin healing our wounds.

Forgiveness opens the door for His goodness to be made real to us.

Personal Processing

Meditate on These Verses

And we know that God causes all things to work together for good to those who love God, to those who are called according to His purpose. For those whom He foreknew, He also predestined to become conformed to the image of His Son, so that He would be the firstborn among many brethren; and these whom He predestined, He also called; and these whom He called, He also justified; and these whom He justified, He also glorified.

—Rom. 8:28–30

Grace to you and peace from God our Father and the Lord Jesus Christ. Blessed be the God and Father of our Lord Jesus Christ, who has blessed us with every spiritual blessing in the heavenly places in Christ, just as He chose us in Him before the foundation of the world, that we would be holy and blameless before Him. In love He predestined us to adoption as sons through Jesus Christ to Himself, according to the kind intention of His will, to the praise of the glory of His grace, which He freely bestowed on us in the Beloved. In Him we have redemption through His blood, the forgiveness of our trespasses, according to the riches of His grace which He lavished on us. In all wisdom and insight He made known to us the mystery of His will, according to His kind intention which He purposed in Him with a view to an administration suitable to the fullness of the times, that is, the summing up of all things in Christ, things in the heavens and things on the earth. In Him also we have obtained an inheritance, having been predestined according to His purpose who works all things after the counsel of His will, to the end that we who were the first to hope in Christ would be to the praise of His glory. In Him, you also, after listening to the message of truth, the gospel of your salvation—having also believed, you were sealed in Him with the Holy Spirit of promise, who is given as a pledge of our inheritance, with a view to the redemption of God's own possession, to the praise of His glory.

—Eph. 1:2–14

1. Read through Ephesians 1:2–14, and write out all the amazing things God did for you that show His goodness to you.

2. Choose a place in your life where you are stuck. Look at the diagram in this chapter and the explanation of the five factors. Process your "stuck

place" with God through the five factors. Take notes of what God showed you and what action you took in response.

3. When you've worked through this, ask the Lord to give you a redemptive picture of yourself.

Prayer

Declare this out loud.

Father, thank You for all the ways You have poured Your goodness out on me. I receive these blessings into the core of my being. Thank You for the supernatural tools You have given me to undo demonic, fallen beliefs in my soul. Thank You that in every factor that influences my life, You have provided a way for me to have victory. I choose to live my life daily communing with You so I can stay alive in Your presence. Amen.

Chapter 7

FORGIVENESS

Surely our griefs He Himself bore,
And our sorrows He carried;
Yet we ourselves esteemed Him stricken,
Smitten of God, and afflicted.
But He was pierced through for our transgressions,
He was crushed for our iniquities;
The chastening for our well-being fell upon Him,
And by His scourging we are healed.

—Isa. 53:4–5

As you've likely perceived by now, the process of the Exchanged life is a radical shift from the way we are used to living, even for many of us as believers. Most of us have lived a life of dependence on ourselves, making our own decisions and dealing with our emotions the best we know how. This is not the way God created us to be. He longs for us to be in constant communion with Him, receiving His love, support, wisdom, and power to live an abundant life. This is my whole foundation for living now. If I didn't have the Lord, I would not know fullness or purpose for all I encounter every day. With the Lord, there is significance in every situation that can produce substance of life with joy and deep satisfaction, causing me to look forward to eternity.

One of the main difficulties for us as humans is the pain that comes in our personal relationships. Much of our lives is about our relationships and how we move through them. God is included in that. Since I was a child, my greatest difficulty has been feeling disappointed by others. As I already shared, I had a lot of disappointment in my family relationships, and the Lord used that to teach me the necessity and value of forgiveness.

Our whole relationship with God is based on His immeasurable love expressed through forgiveness. Adam and Eve chose not to honor Him as God, to worship the creature rather than the Creator, which caused separation from Him. God so loved the world that He gave His only Son to die in our place to pay for that choice and separation. This is the greatest example of forgiveness we could ever experience.

Isaiah 53 says that Christ bore our sin, our sickness, and our pain; He was crushed for our iniquities (generational sin passed down to us), and the punishment for our sin fell on Him. It even says in verse 12 that He was *"numbered with the transgressors."* He actually stood in our place carrying our shame and separation from God so we could have newness of life if we chose Him. Wow! Who does that? God!

Sin is at the root of separation; forgiveness is the healing agent. What makes the process of the Exchange so effective is that it's based on the Lord knowing us intimately and us allowing Him to reveal our "stuck places," the things that separate us from Him and others. He searches us and knows us (Ps. 139) and will reveal the places in us that are choking out His life in and through us. Unforgiveness is the primary "stuck place" in all of us.

. . . .

Unforgiveness is the primary "stuck place" in all of us.

. . . .

What Is Forgiveness?

To forgive is defined like this: "to cease to feel resentment against (an offender); to give up resentment of or claim to requital; to grant relief from payment of."[4]

When we forgive, we need to remember that we also have to receive forgiveness from God. Many times, our inability to receive that forgiveness is why we have a hard time forgiving others. Likewise, if we don't forgive others, the Word says God will not forgive us (Matt. 6:14–15).

Remember that Romans 3:23 says we have sinned and fallen short of the life of God we were intended to dwell in. In our fallenness, God sent His Son to recover what we lost. From a heart of love and reconciliation, He gave His Son to be the propitiation we needed to cover our sin. This is the same heart we are to have. Freely we have received; freely we are to give the same mercy when others sin against us.

---

4. "forgive," *Merriam-Webster*, https://www.merriam-webster.com/dictionary/forgive.

> ### PROPITIATION
>
> *A person, place, or thing that pays the price instead of the debtor to gain or regain favor with another.*
>
> *Romans 3:24–25 says, "[B]eing justified as a gift by His grace through the redemption which is in Christ Jesus, whom God displayed publicly as a propitiation in His blood through faith. This was to demonstrate His righteousness, because in the forbearance of God He passed over the sins previously committed."*

Propitiation is the *sacrifice, the thing that stood in your place.* We deserve to be punished; we were born into the law of sin and death. In reality, we've all believed things, thought things, and done things we deserve punishment for. But in God's unbelievable kindness and grace toward us, the punishment passed over us and went on Him. Jesus Christ is the stand-in. He's the propitiation, the payment for sin on our behalf. He was beaten beyond recognition, nailed to a cross, and humiliated on our behalf. Think about the innocence He carried. He was mocked, He was reviled, He was beaten, He was accused, and yet he was perfect. That blood, that perfect blood, washed and atoned us. It doesn't seem fair, but God isn't about fairness. He's about righteousness and justification. In God's justice and righteousness, He decided it was good to sacrifice His Son in our place so He could have the many for the one.

The Bible has a lot to say about this. Let's look at a few examples.

> *Then Peter came and said to Him, "Lord, how often shall my brother sin against me and I forgive him? Up to seven*

times?" Jesus said to him, "I do not say to you, up to seven times, but up to seventy times seven.

"For this reason the kingdom of heaven may be compared to a king who wished to settle accounts with his slaves. And when he had begun to settle them, one who owed him ten thousand talents was brought to him. But since he did not have the means to repay, his master commanded him to be sold, along with his wife and children and all that he had, and repayment be made. So the slave fell to the ground and prostrated himself before him, saying, 'Have patience with me and I will repay you everything.' And the lord of that slave felt compassion and released him and forgave him the debt. But that slave went out and found one of his fellow slaves who owed him a hundred denarii; and he seized him and began to choke him, saying, 'Pay back what you owe.' So his fellow slave fell to the ground and began to plead with him, saying, 'Have patience with me and I will repay you.' But he was unwilling, and went and threw him in prison until he should pay back what was owed. So when his fellow slaves saw what had happened, they were deeply grieved and came and reported to their lord all that had happened. Then summoning him, his lord said to him, 'You wicked slave, I forgave you all that debt because you pleaded with me. Should you not also have had mercy on your fellow slave, in the same way that I had mercy on you?' And his lord, moved with anger, handed him over to the torturers until he should repay all that was owed him. My heavenly Father will also do the same to you, if each of you does not forgive his brother from your heart."

—Matt. 18:21–35

The slave in this story was forgiven an unpayable debt. An unpayable debt has been paid on our behalf by Jesus. Let's look, though, at how that slave responded to those who owed him. He seized the one and choked him. Wow! Then he threw the offender in prison. That so often describes how we treat those who have offended us or owe us something.

That's exactly what happens spiritually when we refuse to forgive. Not only are we locking up the one we have offense toward, but we are also being locked up because of our unforgiveness. It literally says that this opens the door to torment in the life of the one who will not forgive.

When someone is experiencing recurring bad dreams or some area of their life never seems free from turmoil, most of the time it's connected to unforgiveness. In all the years I've counseled people, I can tell you there have been many in their later years who are struggling with their spouses or a close loved one because they haven't forgiven them. Unforgiveness can taint so much of our life. You do not want to hold on to unforgiveness.

Here's another scripture passage about forgiveness. Colossians 3:13 says, *"[B]earing with one another, and forgiving each other, whoever has a complaint against anyone; just as the Lord forgave you, so also should you."* The Passion Translation words it this way: *"Tolerate the weaknesses of those in the family of faith, forgiving one another in the same way you have been graciously forgiven by Jesus Christ. If you find fault with someone, release this same gift of forgiveness to them."*

Forgiveness is an act of obedience. If for no other reason, we should want to forgive others to demonstrate our submission to God, honoring Him for His forgiveness of us.

"You didn't take the time to anoint my head with fragrant oil, but she anointed my head and feet with the finest perfume. She has been forgiven of all her many sins. This is why she has shown me such extravagant love. But those who assume they have very little to be forgiven will love me very little." Then Jesus said to the woman at his feet, "All your sins are forgiven."

—Luke 7:46–48 (TPT)

In this story of Mary coming to wash Jesus's feet, she breaks an alabaster jar and washes His feet with her tears. Jesus says, *"She has been forgiven of all her many sins. This is why she has shown me such extravagant love"* (Luke 7:47 TPT). Forgiveness produces a deep well of gratitude in us toward God. The more we receive forgiveness for our sin and brokenness, the more the love of God fills us and pours out of us to Him and others. True forgiveness brings a humility in us that lays a God-like foundation for love.

Unforgiveness

What keeps us from wanting to forgive? Some of the top responses are pride, stubbornness, self-righteousness, revenge, and a right-or-wrong mind-set.

To truly forgive, we must check our motives. The Lord knows the true posture of our heart to forgive and whether we are forgiving someone from a place of humility or not. He knows when we're doing it out of self-righteousness. *"GOD IS OPPOSED TO THE PROUD"* (James 4:6).

I've had to forgive countless people throughout my life, as I'm sure you have. Sometimes it's the same person many,

many times. The Lord commands that we forgive seventy times seven, which, by the way, is 490, but He didn't mean for us to take that literally. It means we continually choose to forgive.

There will be times when you don't *want* to forgive a person. In those situations, dialogue with God. Be honest, and tell Him you really don't feel like forgiving that person. That usually happens when we're balancing our scales of self-righteousness instead of seeing God's heart of compassion. Keep talking with your loving heavenly Father and receive His love for you, and before long, your heart will break open and yield to His will, not allowing bitterness to take root in you. God is so patient and long-suffering that He will patiently wait until our hearts and spirits are ready to repent and forgive.

Forgiving someone means we also need to repent. It's not just that the other person needs forgiveness from you, but you also need forgiveness from God for being offended.

We'll talk about offense in the next section. God will soften us and change our will as we press into knowing Him in the place we are struggling to forgive. If we keep relating to God and choosing to yield our will to His, then His will begins to take over. He will remind us how He has forgiven us and that to be like Him, we must forgive. When we let go of our stubbornness and our need to be right, the peace of God begins to flood our mind, will, and emotions. This is the place of oneness with God we want as we live our lives before others. This is where true authority and power begin to manifest in us and through us.

Calista found this place of oneness with God after making an Exchange. When I met with her, she shared with me that she'd grown up in a tumultuous home. Her father was an alcoholic. As an only child, Calista was often caught in the middle of her father's abuse and her mother's role. Calista was an angry child who would sometimes become violent, and she grew to be a rebellious teenager.

As an adult, Calista gave her life to the Lord, and a lot of the outward signs of anger and rebellion faded away. She tried to approach her family with an understanding heart but continued to respond with high levels of anger. No matter how many times she tried to forgive her parents for the pain she had endured at their hands, she could never force her heart to feel differently about them. In the Exchange class, when the forgiveness lesson was taught, Calista felt her heart and mind shut down. She saw all the signs of bitterness in her life—demonic, violent dreams involving her family; jealousy and rage at the sight of a father loving his children; even great difficulty disciplining her own children out of fear of being like him.

As Calista was realizing, forgiveness doesn't happen overnight. Sometimes it can be immediate, but usually we have to be diligent. If we're diligent, it will come. It's not beneficial to put it off. When we push forgiveness aside, time goes by, and we may not realize that the roots of unforgiveness are alive and growing within us. Unforgiveness is where we should check first when we are asking the Lord about strongholds in our lives.

. . . .

Unforgiveness is where we should check first when we are asking the Lord about strongholds in our lives.

. . . .

Hurting one another is a consequence of being in a relationship. It isn't always done intentionally, and there are dozens of coping mechanisms that engage when these conflicts arise. Then strongholds get established. When we experience unforgiveness, it is an open door to seek to know the love of God in a new and fresh way. It is a key way for us to know the love of God again.

The Defilement of Bitterness

Pursue peace with all men, and the sanctification without which no one will see the Lord. See to it that no one comes short of the grace of God; that no root of bitterness springing up causes trouble, and by it many be defiled.

—Heb. 12:14–15

Bitterness enters into our hearts when we hold on to unforgiveness. Bitterness doesn't just affect you and the person you're in conflict with. It spreads and can affect all the relationships in your life. Bitterness taints everything. Bitterness grows out of an offense. An offense is an annoyance or resentment brought about by a perceived insult to or disregard for one's self or one's standards.

Sometimes we do not recognize that we are bitter but will admit to being offended. Harbored offense leads to bitterness. If we do not admit that we are offended, we cannot deal with bitterness. Many times, we are not only offended by people but by the Lord (Matt. 13:53–58; John 6:52–66; 1 Pet. 2:7–8). Proverbs 18:19 says, "*A brother offended is harder to be won than a strong city, and contentions are like the bars of a citadel.*"

Unresolved unforgiveness always leads to bitterness, and bitterness always causes defilement. The defilement isn't just in the relationships of your life but in your mind, will, emotions, and physical body. Unforgiveness puts wear and tear on your body—not only in the form of wrinkles or ulcers, but also medically. Experts have found that bitterness is a major source of diseases and conditions.[5]

Galatians 5:9 says, *"A little leaven leavens the whole lump of dough."* In the Passion Translation, it reads, *"Don't you know that when you allow even a little lie into your heart, it can permeate your entire belief system?"* Like when yeast is activated, the effects of bitterness cannot be hidden or contained. Hymenaeus and Philetus are examples in 2 Timothy 2:16–17 of those who were offended, spreading their worldly chatter like gangrene leading to further ungodliness.

The definition of *defile* is to make unclean or impure; to make physically unclean especially with something unpleasant or contaminating; to violate the sanctity of.[6] It means to pollute as with sin. Bitterness attaches itself to everything a person thinks, says, or does. It transfers to others in ways we cannot account for. Bitterness does not just affect the unforgiven one; it also spreads and contaminates everything. That is why we have to be diligent. Withholding forgiveness isn't just a little secret we have. No, it permeates everything, no matter how hard we try to compartmentalize it. Holding on to bitterness reinforces our soulishness and separates us from God, causing our sensitivity to His voice and ways to be dulled.

---

5. "Forgiveness: Your Health Depends on It," *Johns Hopkins Medicine*, https://www.hopkinsmedicine.org/health/wellness-and-prevention/forgiveness-your-health-depends-on-it.

6. "defile," *Merriam-Webster*, https://www.merriam-webster.com/dictionary/defile.

Calista knew well the consequences of being tainted by unforgiveness. Bitterness and torment reigned in her life after all this time. After several Exchange ministry sessions where she tried to forgive her father, the layers of emotion finally came off, and she got to see her father in the state he truly was in. Calista said God showed her that her father was wrapped in a straitjacket, chained to his own shame and fear of being exposed as not good enough. God showed Calista that she held a key to one of the chains, and as she truly came to understand her father's flaws as God did, she forgave him and unlocked a chain on his straitjacket. It wasn't just that she had to forgive her father out of obligation or because it was the right thing to do; she had to hear what the Lord had to say about her circumstances and receive His perspective. Calista was learning how forgiveness unlocks the love of God and sets us and everyone else involved free to experience Him in His fullness.

Breaking the Power of Bitterness

Breaking the power of bitterness is critical because unforgiveness chains you emotionally and spiritually to the person you won't forgive and gives them power over you even if you don't recognize it. Look at the Forgiveness Diagram. It is a clear depiction of how unforgiveness works. The fact that you are tolerating bitterness keeps you linked to the other person and to the Devil.

Sometimes the obstacle to forgiving someone is our thoughts. *Why should I? They didn't give any regard to me when they were hurting me. What makes you think that when I'm out of the picture, they're going to think twice about me?* They've moved on with their life while you stay stuck. If

I were you, I wouldn't be okay with that. I would pay whatever price I needed to so I could be free and move forward with my life. Forgiveness is the only way to move on.

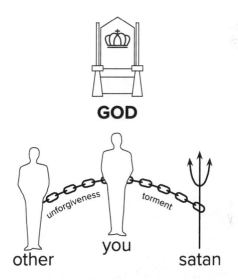

GOD

other   you   satan

Forgiveness Diagram

Bitterness signals to the demonic realm that you are fair game. Unforgiveness also leaves you vulnerable to or chained to the Enemy. It is an open invitation for him to yank your chain or torment you. He may be pulling on the chain, but you're holding the key as to whether you choose to hold on to unforgiveness or unlock yourself from its hold. When you withhold forgiveness, you hand yourself over to torment and torture. Just think about that. You're handing yourself over to the Devil's torment and torture when you choose to hold on to unforgiveness.

As I mentioned before, my mother had a bad temper and was easily angered. I had a lot of unforgiveness and bitterness toward her. It caused me to be easily angered as well and unhappy with life. I became a not so happy person to be around. Because I was a believer, I knew this was a problem, but I justified it as being her problem, not mine.

As I grew in the Lord and desired to be more obedient to Him, He wouldn't let me get away with this. He continued to allow situations to come into my life that forced me to face my unforgiveness. Finally, I decided to unlock this issue through repentance for holding on to the anger and resentment and forgive my mother for the things I felt she had done throughout my life. I was extremely offended. I also had to repent to the Lord for harboring unforgiveness.

Once I worked through all those places with the Lord, it revealed to me that I had unforgiveness toward my dad as well. I was then able to forgive and release him from my expectations just like I had with my mom. Talk about freedom! Years of stuckness. By the way, I had no idea that those issues had caused a lack of self-worth and rejection in me that I was then able to also deal with.

When you hold on to unforgiveness, it causes worth issues in your life, not because of what others did to you but because you are trying to get something from others that you are meant to get primarily from God—being deeply valued.

Remember, a life in the heavenlies means our position is supposed to be as a victor, but unforgiveness keeps us dwelling on what has been done to us and how that offended our value system. It makes us the victim.

When we choose to forgive someone, a good first step is to ask the Lord how He sees them. He'll often show you things that happened to them that made them the way they are, which is probably why they weren't able to give you what you thought they should. That gives you the ability to empathize with the person. Ask God, "What was going on in them that caused them to make those choices that, yes, affected me, but choices that also affected them?" It's a cycle. It may be that this spirit of unforgiveness is present in your family and gets passed on through generations. This cycle needs to stop somewhere, so why not with you and me?

Recognizing Unforgiveness

Some indicators of torment linked to unforgiveness may include the following:

1. Violent or evil dreams

2. Consistent physical pain or sickness

3. Cycles of consistent anger or rage

4. Difficulty sleeping or staying in peace

5. Tormenting thoughts from you, your offspring, or family

Delusions of Unforgiveness

When you expend all your energy holding on to your bitterness, you've taken away your ability to enjoy others and the fullness of Christ. As we've said before, not only does it affect the person you're not forgiving, but it taints much more of your walk with God and others than you realize. It causes us to have an embittered view of life. One of the strongest testimonies of believers' lives is that they love others. You cannot have unforgiveness and love in the same space.

189

Here are some ways that unforgiveness deceives us.

1. Unforgiveness deludes us into thinking we are in control.

2. Unforgiveness deludes us into thinking we are punishing the person who hurt us or that we are protecting ourselves from future pain.

3. Unforgiveness deludes us into thinking we are held to a different standard than the one who hurt us. Let me share something that you may find terrifying. You will be judged by the same standard you are using to judge the one you will not forgive. This delusion produces hypocrisy and death.

Matthew 7:1–2 says, *"Do not judge so that you will not be judged. For in the way you judge, you will be judged; and by your standard of measure, it will be measured to you."* When I'm thinking about how much I want someone to be judged or punished, my next thought is this: *Actually, I wouldn't wish that for myself, so okay, God. I release this to You.*

. . . .

Unforgiveness is always about protecting something.

. . . .

Unforgiveness is always about protecting something. We might think that if we forgive, the other person won't receive what they deserve; but who are we to say what that person deserves? Or we might think if we hold on to unforgiveness, we will be protected from getting hurt again. Unforgiveness does not protect us. It actually leaves us vulnerable. Why? Because we're holding on to a belief that we'll be hurt again. What does that set us up for? Strongholds and repeating cycles.

Galatians 5:6 says, *"For in Christ Jesus neither circumcision nor uncircumcision means anything, but faith working through love."* If we look to God and not man, then we can respond in faith by forgiving and believing the best for the one who hurt us. First Corinthians 13:7 says that love *"bears all things, believes all things, hopes all things, endures all things."* Love always wins—not always with the person but for you with the Lord and others.

When I set myself up as judge by refusing to forgive, it only causes me to suffer. I am not a just judge. We will experience God's justice when we don't forgive because He can't bless us in those places. This will be the one time I'll tell you to be selfish. Don't put off addressing this. You do *not* want to be under God's discipline because you're rebelling against Him; you want to be free. I, for one, do not want to face His discipline toward my rebellious choices. And I don't want you to either. God longs to be the protector of your mind, will, and emotions, but you have to yield to His ways to receive that protection.

The Lord has good boundaries for us. He knows better how to set boundaries and care for us than we do. Often when we don't forgive, we either set really harsh boundaries and are unable to love, or we believe that we somehow have to stay in that painful situation. We can end up being victimized there, not understanding God's love and care for us because we haven't truly forgiven and gotten the Lord's boundaries for our life. Forgiveness is a major part of our coming out of co-dependent patterns with people and coming into true worship and dependence on God. It's after forgiving that we can truly hear from God the true boundaries He wants for us in those relationships.

Let me share a testimony about this. I dated a guy who went to the same church I did. We ran with the same crowd, and we were part of the same prayer gatherings. After a while, that church went through a split. Most of our friends left and began considering starting a new church. The Lord clearly told me I was not to go with them and that I was to stay at the original church.

When I told the guy I was dating about it, he evidently wasn't happy. The next day he left me a note saying I was a white-washed sepulcher and he was breaking up with me. In my soul, I wanted to be mad at him, but after about forty-five seconds, I heard the Lord remind me of Galatians 5:6. He told me that the only choice for me to make to protect my heart and be free was to obey that verse, to believe the best about him, and to love him freely—faith expressing itself through love. In two minutes, I was totally peaceful and full of joy.

True Forgiveness

Eventually we will get tired of holding on to all the bitterness. It's exhausting. We have to be diligent to forgive people in our lives so we can truly be glory carriers, hosts of God's presence, defying all the odds when people come against us.

We must go after these places of bitterness with an unrelenting tenacity. Go to the throne boldly, throw yourself before God in humility, and give Him permission to realign and readjust your heart. Sometimes that's what it takes. Ask the Lord to put the desire of forgiveness in you because you may not feel like doing it. Ask the Lord to humble you. He's usually kinder to us than we are to ourselves. You are not God. It's not your job to hold people accountable for their sin behavior. God is fully able to bring His justice in every situation according to His ways.

Rest in this. God is God, and He will apply justice in the situation and to the person every time, whether we recognize it in the moment or not. No one gets away with anything, but He will handle His judgment in His way, in His time. We have to be open to how God exacts His justice and be okay with what it looks like, even if we think He may have gone easy on the person. You may wish He would bring down the hammer and completely destroy the other person's life, but it probably will not look like that. The other person is His child too. It is His place to bring correction or retribution to that person in a redemptive way, and we must release that part to Him. God is so compassionate but will also bring His righteousness in every situation. You don't want God to be harsh with you, so it's best if we don't want that measure for others.

· · · · · · · · · · · · · · · ·

You don't want God to be harsh with you, so it's best if we don't want that measure for others.

· · · · · · · · · · · · · · · ·

Forgiveness unlocks things that we can't, no matter how hard we might try. After making that Exchange, so much of Calista's personal torment and anger toward her father unraveled. Not surprisingly, her attitude toward herself shifted as well. Remember, bitterness defiles many, and Calista had to see herself as better than others to be able to hold on to her unforgiveness. Truly, God says we will be forgiven as we forgive, and Calista needed to see her need for God's forgiveness as much as she needed to forgive her father. The Lord opened a door in Calista's heart to receive compassion and mercy so she could also give compassion and mercy.

. . . .

It is safe to forgive.

. . . .

Choosing to release unforgiveness is not just for the other person; it's for you too. Forgiveness causes us to know the Lord more deeply and to be able to experience His fullness, His beauty, and His mercy in a whole new way. I've been able to experience the beauty of releasing people and situations and trusting God in my life to take care of me. Hear me on this: it is the highest and best to forgive; it is safe to forgive.

When we forgive, we agree with and release the power of God's forgiveness that He poured out through the cross, reconciling heaven and earth. It's about so much more than our own personal life. We are to stand in the gap between God and man, helping people see who God is. We represent God in all that our lives touch. Second Corinthians 5 calls us ambassadors of God and that we have been given the responsibility to reconcile our part of the world (our daily experiences) to God.

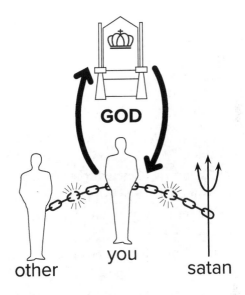

How to Forgive

We begin the process of forgiveness by dialoguing with the Lord. We ask Him, "Lord, how do You see this person? How do You see this situation?" Then agree with the view God shows you. Repent for and renounce any place where you do not agree with God. Say, "God, I come out of agreement with unforgiveness. I choose not to align with unforgiveness." Choose to forgive them and bless them.

Ephesians 4:30–32 says, *"Do not grieve the Holy Spirit of God, by whom you were sealed for the day of redemption. Let all bitterness and wrath and anger and clamor and slander be put away from you, along with all malice. Be kind to one another, tender-hearted, forgiving each other, just as God in Christ also has forgiven you."* When we truly love someone, we don't want to grieve them. We don't want to intentionally or purposefully do something that hurts them. Because we love God and the Holy Spirit is in us, we don't want to grieve them. We can say to the Holy Spirit, "I do not want to grieve You. So empower me to forgive, to let go, to release, to yield to You." That's what it comes down to. Do you trust Him?

To offer true forgiveness is not just saying to the Lord, "I forgive this person." It's an interaction with the person as well, if they know you are offended. The Word tells us to go to them and tell them the Lord has shown you your offense and you want to let them know you have repented of the offense and have released them.

What can sometimes trip a person up in their work to forgive is the need for their position to be understood. "I forgive you, but I want you to know why I thought that way or why that hurt me." But explaining yourself isn't always helpful. Holding on for the chance to explain is just another form of holding on to try to be right. The other person doesn't need to have the full story. It's enough that God knows.

Whether or not they receive you isn't your concern. Your concern is to go to them. The forgiven person does not need to understand you or agree with you. This is about you releasing them for your own obedience to God.

Sometimes the person may act like he or she isn't listening to you. We can't control how a person responds. Our job is to answer as unto the Lord. We can extend and release forgiveness to the person whether or not they accept it, whether or not they think they need it. If you don't have access to resolve it with the person directly, it's okay. Release the situation to the Lord, and ask Him to resolve it and heal the relationship.

Unforgiveness enslaves us to the Enemy and defiles our life through bitterness. When we choose to hold on to unforgiveness, it affects us in ways we may not even realize. It isn't only affecting us; it is also affecting our relationships. Unforgiveness doesn't punish the person you have unforgiveness toward; it brings you hurt and separation from God's desire for you to live in His fullness through Christ.

Scripture tells us we will be forgiven in the same measure that we forgive others. If we let go of feeling like we have to control the outcome, we can release the situation to God who is sovereign, who loves us unconditionally, and who promises that justice will prevail. Forgiving is a powerful biblical action that unlocks the Holy Spirit's ability to bring healing and deliverance to us.

Forgiveness releases God's glory on the earth and reconciles earth to heaven. Amazing! We get to participate in bringing heaven to earth on a regular basis just by forgiving others. Let's agree to be quick repenters and forgivers. Let's not allow the Devil's schemes to entrap us from experiencing and releasing the love of God daily.

Christ came to set captives free. Hopefully you have been set free through receiving God's forgiveness of your sin through Christ's shed blood on the cross and His resurrection from the dead. If not, you can receive Him right now as Savior and Lord by praying this prayer:

Father, I realize now that I am a sinner and live life my own way. I recognize that I was created to live life in communion with You. I repent for going my own way and ask You to forgive me. I invite You to come into my life and be my Lord. I yield everything to You. Thank You for saving me. Amen.

If you're already a believer (or are now because you prayed that prayer), be sure to look at the What's Next section at the end of the book.

Personal Processing

Meditate on These Verses

Then Peter came up and said to Him, "Lord, how often shall my brother sin against me and I forgive him? Up to seven times?" Jesus said to him, "I do not say to you, up to seven times, but up to seventy times seven.

"For this reason the kingdom of heaven may be compared to a king who wished to settle accounts with his slaves. When he had begun to settle them, one who owed him ten thousand talents was brought to him. But since he did not have the means to repay, his lord commanded him to be sold, along with his wife and children and all that he had, and repayment to be made. So the slave fell to the ground and prostrated himself before him, saying, 'Have patience with me and I will repay you everything.' And the lord of that slave felt compassion and released him and forgave him the debt. But that slave went out and found one of his fellow slaves who owed him a hundred denarii; and he seized him and began to choke him, saying, 'Pay back what you owe.' So his fellow slave fell to the ground and began to plead with him, saying, 'Have patience with me and I will repay you.' But he was unwilling and went and threw him in prison until he should pay back what was owed.

So when his fellow slaves saw what had happened, they were deeply grieved and came and reported to their lord all that had happened. Then summoning him, his lord said to him, 'You wicked slave, I forgave you all that debt because you pleaded with me. Should you not also have had mercy on your fellow slave, in the same way that I had mercy on you?' And his lord, moved with anger, handed him over to the torturers until he should repay all that was owed him. My heavenly Father will also do the same to you, if each of you does not forgive his brother from your heart."

—Matt. 18:21–35

[B]earing with one another, and forgiving each other, whoever has a complaint against anyone; just as the Lord forgave you, so also should you.

—Col. 3:13

Pursue peace with all men, and the sanctification without which no one will see the Lord. See to it that no one comes short of the grace of God; that no root of bitterness springing up causes trouble, and by it many be defiled.

—Heb. 12:14–15

Let all bitterness and wrath and anger and clamor and slander be put away from you, along with all malice. Be kind to one another, tender-hearted, forgiving each other, just as God in Christ also has forgiven you.

—Eph. 4:31–32

1. Make a list of the strongholds the Lord has revealed to you. Now make a list of all the people you have unforgiveness toward.

2. Journal about who you are not ready to forgive, and begin a dialogue with God about that.

3. Pull out your Bible, and read each of the key verses above. In your journal, write down some phrases that stuck out to you in each passage.

4. Go back to your list of those you have unforgiveness toward. According to God's Word, forgive them, and release them to the Lord.

Prayer

Declare this out loud.

Lord Jesus, I submit to Your lordship right now in the totality of my heart. You are the only Righteous Judge. I confess I have no right to hold judgment over anyone in my life. I ask You to reveal to me right now any person I am holding unforgiveness toward—even if it's You—and show me all the ways that unforgiveness has affected me. I commit to walk through this process of true forgiveness with You. I want to be freed. Amen.

A WORD OF ENCOURAGEMENT

Habakkuk 2:14 says that the knowledge of the glory of the Lord will fill the earth. That glory is coming through you and me when we allow God to fill us with His glory. Imagine in your mind all believers being filled up with the glory of God, covering the earth. That's God's intention.

> *He made from one man every nation of mankind to live on all the face of the earth, having determined their appointed times and the boundaries of their habitation, that they would seek God, if perhaps they might grope for Him and find Him, though He is not far from each one of us; for in Him we live and move and exist, as even some of your own poets have said, "For we also are His children."*
>
> *—Acts 17:26–28*

When we grope for Him and find Him, His glory manifests in us. Each believer doing that is the fulfillment of Habakkuk 2:14. Your life circumstances are the way God creates in you the desire to grope for Him. He has set you in boundaries to stir up your yearning to know Him and increase in Him.

"For I know the plans that I have for you," declares the LORD, *"plans for welfare and not for calamity to give you a future and a hope. Then you will call upon Me and come and pray to Me, and I will listen to you. You will seek Me and find Me when you search for Me with all your heart. I will be found by you,"* declares the LORD, *"and I will restore your fortunes and will gather you from all the nations and from all the places where I have driven you,"* declares the LORD, *"and I will bring you back to the place from where I sent you into exile."*

—Jer. 29:11–14

This is God's promise for those who will search for Him.

I pray for you to be a child of God who hungers and thirsts for Him in this way. I pray that you will pay the price to lay down your life for His glory.

WHAT'S NEXT?

All resources are offered in person and virtually. You can participate from anywhere in the world.

The Exchange Class
This eight-week class covers the Exchange Message in depth, giving more practical applications to what you've read in this book.

Facilitator Training
You can become a certified and paid Exchange Facilitator through the Launch Institute training track. This course includes classroom and practicum hours. Exchange Facilitators can work flexible hours and lead in-person or virtual sessions through the Exchange Center.

For more information, visit launchinstitute.org
Questions? E-mail us at info@launchinstitute.org

Exchange Ministry Sessions
Are you interested in experiencing a ministry session like the ones you've read about? Each ministry session is a facilitator-led conversation between you and the Lord to discover His truth for your life.

For more information, visit theexchangecenter.org
Questions? E-mail us at info@theexchangecenter.org

BIBLIOGRAPHY

"Forgiveness: Your Health Depends on It." *Johns Hopkins Medicine.* https://www.hopkinsmedicine.org/health/wellness-and-prevention/forgiveness-your-health-depends-on-it.

Murray, Andrew. 2017. *The Power of the Blood of Jesus.* Abbotsford: Aneko Press.

Nee, Watchman. 1968. *The Spiritual Man.* Richmond: Christian Fellowship Publishers.

ADDITIONAL RESOURCES

Billheimer, Paul E. 1982. *Destined for the Cross*. Carol Stream, IL: Tyndale House Publishers.

Billheimer, Paul E. 1975. *Destined for the Throne*. Minneapolis: Bethany House.

Bonhoeffer, Dietrich. 1995. *The Cost of Discipleship*. New York: Touchstone.

Grubb, Norman P. 2016. *Rees Howells: Intercessor*. Fort Washington, PA: CLC Publications.

Grubb, Norman P. 2007. *Touching the Invisible*. CLC Ministries.

Guyon, Jeanne. 1981. *Experiencing the Depths of Jesus Christ*. Sargent, GA: SeedSowers.

Guyon, Jeanne. 1981. *Union with God*. Sargent, GA: SeedSowers.

Nee, Watchman. 1977. *The Normal Christian Life*. Carol Stream, IL: Tyndale House Publishers.

Nee, Watchman. 2000. *The Release of the Spirit*. New York: Christian Fellowship Publishers.

ACKNOWLEDGMENTS

Thank you . . .

To God the Father for making a way of redemption and fullness for us through His Son.

To my mom, who saw my destiny long before I did and gave her best to encourage me in it.

To Eric and Rebecca Vaughn, who labored with me in the foundations of the Exchange Ministries sessions and teachings.

To Sonja Bomhoff, Tom and Wendy Dermott, and Steve Fish for giving opportunity for the first teaching, training, and development of this message.

To Kerri Shepard for picking up the mantle, and to all those who became ministry facilitators in Ft. Worth, Houston, Mexico, and Bosnia, expanding the reach of the message.

To the team who helped me get this life message into a book—Cynthia Wenz, Rebecca Strayer, Kerri Shepard, Evie Swayne, and a host of others from Launch Houston.

To all of you who have taken classes, taught classes, and are on the journey of living a life yielded to God!